A Life CHANGED BY Love

A Life CHANGED BY Love

Change;
the Key that Unlocked My Chains

Victoria Lynn King

Pleasant Word
A Division of WINEPRESS PUBLISHING

Printed in the United States of America

Packaged by Pleasant Word, a division of WinePress Publishing, PO Box 428, Enumclaw, WA 98022. The views expressed or implied in this work do not necessarily reflect those of Pleasant Word, a division of WinePress Publishing. Ultimate design, content, and editorial accuracy of this work are the responsibilities of the author.

ISBN 1-57921-586-6
Library of Congress Catalog Card Number: 2003100415

Table of Contents

Introduction

I felt an overwhelming heaviness in my spirit. I thought why, what does this mean? I cried out to God in prayer. "God what's the matter with me?" You have to prepare yourself for his response when you ask that question. During that prayer time I realized the significance of a specific date in the upcoming month. That month was February and that date was the 14th. Valentine's Day is the day to demonstrate and profess love. Television and magazine advertisements for balloons, candy, perfume, and roses etc. begin the first week in the New Year. This was the day that's set aside to show that special person(s) in your life how much you care. Romantic dinners are prepared using tailored menus to ensure everything being just right for the loved one. Some have waited until that date to marry. Those thoughts made my feeling of spiritual heaviness seem inappropriate. After all, I wasn't expecting anything. I was now at a place where all I wanted and needed was Jesus.

Yet that feeling of heaviness didn't cease. It just didn't seem to make sense. I've found that God's purpose isn't to make sense (to us); he purposes to make saints (of us)!

I realized that many people don't love themselves; therefore they are unable to demonstrate, give, and/or receive love. When you don't have a significant, or any, other you may experience a feeling of hopelessness. Some, in what they thought to be a significant relationship, experience a reality check. I'm aware that everyone isn't romantic and that some may be in a loving relationship and still not receive any acknowledgment on Valentine's Day. However, in either case, it's disappointing when you don't receive what you believed you should and more importantly would.

The reason I felt that heaviness in my spirit was because God allowed me to feel the pain associated with that day. I felt his desire for single people to know that he loved them, unconditionally, without hesitation or reservation. His love is the best and the greatest love. Once you've experienced his love, you're not easily depressed, disappointed, discouraged, disgruntled or dismayed by what you may not receive from man on Valentine's or any other day. You'll have the inward feeling of knowing you're loved and that knowledge will sustain you. The following scripture is foundational for my book "A Life Changed by Love." Ephesians 3:19: *"and to know the love of Christ, which passeth knowledge, that ye might be filled with all the fullness of God."* The reason the love of Christ passeth knowledge is because his love is everywhere; around us, behind us, beside us, in front of us, over us, under us, through us, and what still blows my mind is the fact that it's in us (Glory to God!). The Psalmist says it best in Psalm 139:6: *Such knowledge is too wonderful for me; it is high I cannot attain unto it*. I agree with the Psalmist however I've made knowing and then operating in the love of God a goal for my life.

This desire to share God's love on Valentine's Day was so real that I decided to have a Valentine's Day gathering for singles. God helped me therefore I secured a place (Thank you Aunt Lillian), prepared invitations, food, and obtained music for the gathering. I mailed approximately twenty invitations. They were beautiful; I used red paper with a black heart border. I worked for Gibson Greeting Cards, Inc. and found what I believe to be their best card. I placed the wording from the card on the front of my invitation. It read:

Dear Friend,

I just wanted to tell you that I care about you. It might surprise you if you knew just how much. I know you have so many things on your mind and I'd love to share those things with you— whether it's helping you face the tough times or celebrating with you when everything's going great. I've been waiting a long time to prove my friendship to you, but I won't push. I'll be here for you, because I love you.

Your friend,
Jesus

How appropriate! I made sure that the invitation would be received in the invitee's mailbox on Valentine's Day. My heart was so full of the love that God wanted to express to his people. Well to my dismay, no one came. (Hopefully they had gone on dates). I was so disappointed. All I had wanted was to give love and yet it wasn't received by the many I invited. As I sat in that place with all the fixings, I again cried out to God. "Lord, I know you wanted me to do this, where is everybody?" He taught me three very valuable lessons there. The first was that I was now feeling what he's often felt. He has already provided everything we need for life and life more abundantly and yet the way to destruction is still broad. It's heart wrenching when you've provided everything (not just some things) and become aware that it's been overlooked and not heeded to. You see many seek A blessing, but not THE blessing, which is Jesus. They seek his hand but not his face. Jesus, isn't just a Spiritual Santa Clause dispersing earthly and heavenly gifts to his children, he's the Saviour!

Secondly he showed me that, when dealing with man, obedience to God's purpose doesn't always guarantee success. He said they rejected me, what made you think they would receive you? At that point because of those valuable spiritual nuggets, I felt my event had been very successful. I'd learned that the blessing was and is his presence. You never ever walk away from the presence of God empty handed. His presence is the present! Oftentimes God's blessings don't come the way we think they should. The blessing is and comes from our being obedient to him. One thing that isn't heeded to, as it should be, is obedience to the good, acceptable and perfect will and way of God identified in the word of God. I dried my tears, and began to gather my belongings to go home. As I prepared to leave, the Lord sent someone. She came with my sister Denyse. Thank God for family. Her name is Denisa. God is a wonder because I wouldn't have invited her since she's married.

She seemed to enjoy herself and prayerfully she was blessed by the word we shared. The third thing that God showed me was that everybody needs love regardless of marital status. Oftentimes we offer help to those we think need it. However there may be a greater need for help by someone who doesn't appear helpless.

I hope you already know how much God loves you, but if not, I pray that after reading this book, you will.

FYI

Scripture(s) are best understood relative to surrounding scripture(s). That ensures accurate understanding of the message given. My book will only reference the name of the book and the chapter number i.e. Genesis 1. It doesn't include the number(s) of the written verse(s). I recommend reading the entire chapter(s). Although it may or may not be in the verse(s) that I'm referring to I believe that God will reveal himself to you in a special way!

> Proverbs 25: "It is the glory of God to conceal a thing but the honour of kings to search out a matter."

God gets the glory when we find that concealed thing while searching out a matter.

(All scriptures are taken from the King James Version of the Holy Bible)

Be blessed!

Chapter 1

Love: Leader Over Victorious Events

During that period of time, the Lord gave me an Acronym for the word Love: **Leader Over Victorious Events.**

L et me define my understanding of a Victorious Event. It's one that produces God's will in your life and reaches out to embrace the lives of others. As I considered that acronym, the first example that came to me was John 3: *For God so loved the world that he gave his only begotten Son, that whosoever believeth in him should not perish, but have everlasting life.* Then I considered 1 John 4: *Herein is love, not that we loved God, but that he loved us and sent his Son to be the propitiation for our sins.* Jesus dying to save a wretch like me demonstrated love leading a very victorious event. Love leads; it shouldn't follow! In other words it should be the first and not the last thing you do. A victorious event's primary objective ISN'T its own comfort.

I began to think about the many illustrations in the book called the Bible. Let's look at a few of them. Gen. 1: *In the beginning God created the heaven and the earth.* Love creates yet doesn't dominate. *So God created man in his own image, in the image of God created he him; male and female created he them. And God blessed them, and God said unto them, Be fruitful, and multiply, and replenish the earth, and subdue it: and have dominion over the fish of the sea, and over the fowl of the air, and over every living thing that moveth upon the earth.* Love says nothing less than the best for my blessed! *And God saw every thing that he had made and, behold, it was very good.* Love makes everything very good! *And the evening and the morning were the sixth day.* I was getting excited and decided to look for more examples. I didn't have to go to another book, but only a chapter or two. Genesis 3 speaks about the fall of man due to his disobedience. My defense of Eve would be that any time you receive second hand knowledge the impact of that knowledge is lessened. The person given first hand knowledge has the greatest account-ability for keeping the constraint of that knowledge. Eve was deceived, but Adam decided.

As I read the bible, I understood that God has an order. Man was supposed to provide to and for woman, not the other way around. Disorder usually results in disaster! That understanding alone may give encouragement to someone who was cast aside because they chose not to take care of a man. In some cases this man may even be a grown son. Genesis 3: *And when the woman saw that the tree was good for food, and that it was pleasant to the eyes, and a tree to be desired to make one wise, she took of the fruit thereof, and did eat, and gave also unto her husband with her; and he did eat. And the eyes of them both were opened, and they knew that they were naked; and they sewed fig leaves together, and made themselves aprons. And they heard the voice of the LORD God walking in the garden in the cool of the day: and Adam and his wife hid themselves from the presence of the LORD God amongst the trees of the garden. And the LORD God called unto Adam, and said unto him, Where art thou? And he said, I heard thy voice in the garden, and I was afraid, because I was naked; and I hid myself. And he said, Who told thee that thou wast naked? Hast thou eaten of the tree, whereof I commanded thee that thou shouldest not eat? And the man said, The woman whom thou gavest to be with me, she gave me of the tree, and I did eat.* Now back to my point. Gen. 3: *Unto Adam also and to his wife did the LORD God make coats of skins, and clothed them.* God is so good, even when we mess up his love provides for us. Love provides no matter what.

That fact isn't surprising when you understand Abraham's prophetic statement. Let me inform you of something. This prophetic statement blesses me and you will read it more than once in this book. Most people focus on the whole verse. This verse is excellent, but there are four words in this verse which minister to me. I know them to be true for I've seen it over and over again in my life, Hallelujah! Gen. 22: *And Abraham said, My son, <u>God will provide himself</u> a lamb for a burnt offering.* Yes, Mary Had A Little Lamb! We live in a world where delegation is the norm. The person highest in authority approves (in some cases develops) a strategy and gives it to others to implement. But look at God, who provided himself then and is still providing himself. John 15: *I am the vine, ye are the branches: He that abideth in me, and I in him, the same bringeth forth much fruit: for without me ye can do nothing.*

This principle is all throughout the bible. I remember the story that really opened my eyes to how applicable the word of God is. This story touched me because I had experienced what I thought to be a similar occurrence. A car struck my son approximately fifteen years ago. I was so distraught that the paramedic leaned down to me (laying out in the street beside Tony) and said "Ms., can you get up so that we can help the patient?" I wasn't even hit, but you would've thought I was. I can only imagine what Tony must have thought about my actions. After all, I wasn't the one hit, he was. This bible story illustrates meekness, strength under control, and the necessary actions for victory. Let's take a look.

II Kings 4: *And he said, What then is to be done for her? And Gehazi answered, Verily she hath no child, and her husband is old. And he said, Call her. And when he had called her, she stood in the door. And he said, About this season, according to the time of life, thou shalt embrace a son. And she said, Nay, my lord, thou man of God, do not lie unto thine handmaid. And the woman conceived, and bare a son at that season that Elisha had said unto her, according to the time of life. And when the child was grown, it fell on a day that he went out to his father to the reapers. And he said unto his father, My head, my head! And he said to a lad, Carry him to his mother.*

Some men still take their sick child to his/her mother.

And when he had taken him, and brought him to his mother, he sat on her knees till noon, and then died.

I felt that Tony's situation was tragic and it wasn't. However the bible declares that this child had died in his mother's arms!

I couldn't handle Tony being hit by a car. His dying in my arms would be unbearable! Look at how she handled herself and this situation.

And she went up, and laid him on the bed of the man of God, and shut the door upon him, and went out.

If you read the entire chapter you'll recall that she'd made this bed for the man she perceived to be of God.

God may use the very thing you gave to bless someone else to bless you!

And she called unto her husband, and said, Send me, I pray thee, one of the young men, and one of the asses, that I may run to the man of God, and come again. And he said, Wherefore wilt thou go to him today? it is neither new moon, nor sabbath.

Look at her composure. It's obvious she wasn't visibly upset. Her husband was curious, but not overly concerned, about her actions.

And she said, It shall be well.

Oh my God! What a woman of faith. Her son had died in her arms and this is what she said. She indicated that it wasn't well but she believed it would be well. Then I remembered how I reacted when Tony was struck and I felt about two feet tall.

Then she saddled an ass, and said to her servant, Drive, and go forward; slack not thy riding for me, except I bid thee.

You have to know where to go and while you're on your way, run and don't let anyone or anything hinder you!

So she went and came unto the man of God to mount Carmel. And it came to pass, when the man of God saw her afar off, that he said to Gehazi his servant, Behold, yonder is that Shunammite: run now, I pray thee, to meet her, and say unto her, Is it well with thee? is it well with thy husband? is it well with the child? And she answered, It is well.

Always speak positive words as you make your way to the man of God. Many times we give T.M.I. (too much information) to the wrong people!

Only discuss your problem with the one who can do something about it.

And when she came to the man of God to the hill, she caught him by the feet: but Gehazi came near to thrust her away. And the man of God said, let her alone; for her soul is vexed within her: and the LORD hath hid it from me, and hath not told me. Then she said, Did I desire a son of my lord? did I not say, Do not deceive me?

You can remind God about his promise to you.

Be willing to stand (firm) for and on that promise no matter how dead your situation appears.

Then he said to Gehazi, Gird up thy loins, and take my staff in thine hand, and go thy way: if thou meet any man, salute him not; and if any salute thee, answer him not again: and lay my staff upon the face of the child. And the mother of the child said, As the LORD liveth, and as thy soul liveth, I will not leave thee. And he arose, and followed her.

It's always better to stay with the man of God!

And Gehazi passed on before them, and laid the staff upon the face of the child; but there was neither voice, nor hearing. Wherefore he went again to meet him, and told him, saying, The child is not awaked.

If she had gone with Gehazi, then she would've had to come again to Elisha. Again, it's always better to stay with the man of God until you've received your deliverance.

And when Elisha was come into the house, behold, the child was dead, and laid upon his bed. He went in therefore, and shut the door upon them twain, and prayed unto the LORD. And he went up, and lay upon the child, and put his mouth upon his mouth, and his eyes upon his eyes, and his hands upon his hands: and he stretched himself upon the child; and the flesh of the child waxed warm. Then he returned, and walked in the house to and fro; and went up, and stretched himself upon him: and the child sneezed seven times, and the child opened his eyes. And he called Geha'zi, and said, Call this Shunammite. So he called her. And when she was come in unto him, he said, Take up thy son. Then she went in, and fell at his feet, and bowed herself to the ground, and took up her son, and went out.

Her victory was obtained with her first response of "It shall be well." Her priorities were right. She put first things first.

This text identifies that Love was the Leader Over Victorious Events because in this story, the Shunammite's love for her child, her husband and her respect and honor for the man of God:

1). provided calmness in the midst of her crisis.
2). provided strength at a time when weakness would have been acceptable.
3). provided new life (Victorious Event) for her son even though death had been present.

4). provided a personal intimate knowledge of God's power.

Proverbs 24: *Then I saw, and considered it well: I looked upon it, and received instruction.*

I obviously needed to make some changes in my life and move from religion to relationship!

Please understand that the end result, the Victorious Event, isn't going to be easily obtained. Jesus paid it all but there are still things we must do also. Our willingness to daily crucify our flesh by being obedient to the word of God should be our main objective.

As I considered this principle I began to think of situations in my life. The first one I thought of was when I found out that my daughter had Scoliosis. It was October 13, 1997. That day didn't start out good. My daughter woke up with her right eye slightly closed. I realized that I couldn't send her to school with what I knew to be pink eye. I had to take her to the doctor. I called the doctor's office and was told that her doctor wouldn't be in the office, however his assistant would see her. That assistant was only seeing patients in the Loveland Office. At that point in my life I was a Montgomery Road only person. My sister, Niecie, kept telling me that I needed to venture out. I did; sometimes while driving on Montgomery Rd I'd make a left or a right. I was pretty sure that Loveland wasn't on Montgomery Rd. We took (what seemed to be) the long journey to the Loveland office.

When we got into his office, he proceeded to examine her.

He lifted the back of her shirt to listen to her breathing. I was sitting across from her. I thought I traveled here for pink eye. Now I'm no doctor, but I know where her eye is and that's not where. I guess my flesh was still responding to the trip to Loveland and the thought of the journey back home. When he finished listening to her breathing he lowered her shirt and calmly asked the dreadful question "How long has she had Scoliosis?" I looked at him with amazement. I replied that I wasn't aware that she had Scoliosis. Since I was sitting across from her, he again lifted the back of her shirt and asked her to bend over. I then saw the hump on her right shoulder. I was dumbfounded. My feelings fluctuated between this can't be happening to I'm a bad mother for not realizing this before. By now, I had forgotten all about the pink eye. I was very thankful for the trip to Loveland and the extensive examination. I'm not sure her doctor would've been as alert. After all, she had the same doctor for years and he hadn't noticed. The doctor gave me a prescription to get the necessary medication for pink eye. He then suggested I get a referral to an Orthopedic Doctor for further examination. Life would never be the same again!

I contacted my doctor for the referral and was given the name of Dr. Alvin Crawford. I then scheduled an appointment with Dr. Crawford. Anxiety, apprehension and nervousness attacked me as I sat in the waiting room. I had been praying, ever since I learned of the dreaded "S" word. I prayed that we'd get there and find that this was a bad dream. After what seemed to be an eternity, we were ushered in to see Dr. Crawford. He explained that depending on the degree of the curve, Scoliosis could be treated with a corrective brace. Thank you Jesus. However his examination of her revealed that her curvature was already 40 degrees. She still had a few more years to grow. If not corrected that curvature would do so also. She would HAVE to have back surgery. I wanted to faint but had to keep my composure for her sake. He continued to explain that it would be a five—six hour surgery where they would put two rods in her back. He went on to say that this type of surgery would need a lot of preparation. She'd need at least six months of monthly exams and to donate blood. Her donated blood would be refrigerated and then given to her during her surgery. The fact that she'd receive her own blood provided me with a sense of comfort. When I finally got to my secret place I cried and cried and cried out to God.

During that prayer time God showed me his provision. Prior to finding out about the Scoliosis I had really been seeking God's presence and power in my life. I had been baptized in Jesus name, for the remission of my sins, at Greater Emanuel Apostolic Temple. However I hadn't received the Holy Ghost evidenced by the speaking in other tongues at the Spirit's utterance. On Sunday, October 12, 1997, I cried out to God to receive the gift of the Holy Ghost. I was attending an AME church at that time. That morning I told God that I was going back to Greater Emanuel. I wasn't leaving there without the Holy Ghost. After service, I went to the young lady who had assisted in my baptism and asked if she would tarry with me for the Holy Ghost. She didn't remember me, but I remembered her. She hastily consented and her excitement heightened my desire to receive. Thanks Sister Elaine Wilmore. Don't ever feel that your good works are futile. God has a way of bringing those things back to remembrance, long after you've forgotten about the impact you've made in someone's life. I believe that's purposed to keep us humble. God blessed me with the power of the Holy Ghost with the evidence of speaking in tongues that Sunday. I didn't know why I felt such a strong desire for his power on that particular day; he knew I'd need it. I am so grateful. There's no provision like God's provision!

I didn't know anything about Orthopedics but everyone keep telling me how blessed I was to have Dr. Crawford as her surgeon. He's considered the best by his peers and has traveled all around the world doing this type of surgery. When I inquired about an Orthopedic Surgeon I wasn't aware of who was the best. I just wanted her to see an Orthopedic Doctor. God is so good. That provision was given to me. During the time prior to her surgery, I prayed a lot and purchased "healing" books. I believed that God could heal her without surgery. I'm sure my daughter tired of those daily rubs with my anointing oil. Sometimes life presents a situation where you're willing to do anything and everything for your victory. I had NO SHAME IN MY GAME as I attempted to deliver my daughter from the dreaded "S"!

Unfortunately that never happened. I couldn't understand why she had to have surgery. I understood Dr. Crawford's explanation, but why didn't I find out about it before the curvature had advanced to this degree? All types of crazy thoughts came to mind. I even considered suing her doctors. Finally I realized that wouldn't change the fact that she needed the surgery. Still the fact that this decision was taken away from me really bothered me. Why wasn't I able to choose? I preferred that she wear a corrective brace for a period of months.

During one of her monthly doctor visits the screening nurse examined Kaneeka. She casually mentioned that a friend of hers was also diagnosed with Scoliosis as a teenager. However, at that time, her degree of curvature was only about 25. Therefore her parent's had a choice and they decided against the surgery. That friend was now in her early thirties and pregnant. She had endured severe pain because of the Scoliosis and would have that surgery after her baby was born. She wishes she had the surgery as a teenager. Although my heart went out to her, I was so grateful and thankful to God for taking that decision away from me. That's when I finally understood the reason that choice was taken from me. I knew that I also would have chosen to wait. Kaneeka's surgery, just like that woman's, was inevitable. God's love again proved to be the leader over a victorious event.

I thank God for the later on's in my life. Many times we don't understand why things happen as they do. God knows the end from the beginning. So now, almost five years later, again I say Thank God for his Love, which always leads us in the Victorious way! God just gave me another thought. I had to travel a far distance to Love-land to receive the help I really needed. We must be willing to go outside our comfort zone to receive total deliverance. Glory!!!!! Love-land, (where Jesus resides), is the only place you can receive what you need!

Love: Leader Over Victorious Events

Father God,

My prayer for this reader is that you would allow them to remember all the Victorious Events you've provided in their lives. I pray that once they do so, that remembrance will produce an overwhelming love and desire for you and your desired will for their life.

In Jesus Name,
Amen

Chapter 2

A Life Changed By Love

I chose this title for my book because it identified what God's presence has done in my life. His love gave me the courage and the willingness needed to change and that change released the chains of bondage from my life. Where do I start to illustrate my first understanding of this principle? I'll start with my earliest memories of a life changed by love. My parents divorced when my sister and I were young. At first we lived with my mom. Divorce was difficult for her. Yet she always put her love for us ahead of her needs. We lived with different family members. We moved around a lot. It seemed like every month. Later I found out why. My mom never wanted her family to be a burden to anyone. Anytime someone even hinted that we were bothersome or in the way she sought another place for us to live. She was willing to uproot her life at the drop of a hat because of her love for my sister and I.

My dad was always in our life. He lived in Brooklyn. I loved the train rides to his house. Well I did until I fractured my wrist inside one of the cars. Our moving around bothered him. He felt that we needed a more stabilized home life. Therefore he decided to purchase a house in Cambria Heights, N.Y. My mom was heartbroken when she realized what my dad was going to do. However she also wanted us to have our own home so she allowed us to move in with him. My dad was a single parent in the seventies. That was unusual because back then single parenting wasn't as prevalent or done by a man. His life was drastically changed. He now had the daily responsibility of raising his two young daughters. I was the cook. Notice I didn't say I was an experienced cook, but I did my best. Every Thursday we'd go out to dinner. We began to go out more frequently. My dad would call about 4 P.M. and ask, "Baby, have you started cooking yet?" I'd reply, "Not yet Daddy and he'd say "Well you don't have to; we'll go out tonight." I noticed that he starting calling earlier and earlier. When he called at 9 A.M. I began to realize that perhaps he didn't (really) like my cooking. After all, who starts cooking dinner that early? Niecie would say "Lynn, I love it when you're supposed to cook; we always get to go out." My second memory of a life changed by love was living with my Dad.

When I was pregnant with Tony my brothers, Rondo and Donald, would come into my room every night to rub my stomach. They were so excited about their new nephew or niece. Their lives were changed by love for a child they'd never seen. The bigger my stomach grew, the bigger their smiles grew. Now that I think about it, I wonder if they were smiling with me or smiling at (all) of me? I'll have to check with them and get back to you! The pains started on April 7. This was a different type of pain. My rear end felt as if it would explode from all the pressure. I tried to endure the pain, but my strategy wasn't working. The first time we arrived at the hospital they sent me home. They reasoned that I hadn't dilated enough. I knew I had dilated enough, (I was bugging out), however the nurse insisted that my eyes weren't the area of concern.

I returned and gave birth on April 8, 1978 @ 2:32 PM to a beautiful baby boy. We both weighed the same amount at birth: 6 lbs., 14 oz. I named him Tony. What a joy. I can't describe my feelings as I looked at him. He was such a cutie. He had curly black hair. Most of the time people thought he was a little girl. And guess what, almost 25 years later, the love he manifested in my heart is still changing my life. I've experienced emotions that I'd never known before he came into my life. I love you Son. Thank you for being one of the greatest parts of me.

My daughter was born on August 1, 1984 @ 6:27 P.M. Her birth time was the month and date of my birth (June 27th). That pregnancy and delivery had been very difficult. Due to a massive hemorrhage I had an emergency C-Section. By that time we'd both gone through so much. She was born premature at almost 28 weeks. She'd struggled to get here. I knew she was going to be a fighter. I didn't think my heart could embrace any more love. However, when I looked at my beautiful little girl. What can I say? I had been raising a son for six years before she came along. She had (and still has) very long hair. I humorously said "Lord,

I wasn't even doing hair, now you've given me Rapunzel."
When she was little, Tony was so funny. He'd heard us
refer to her as premature (or a preemie). If I commented
about anything that she'd done, he'd reply (in her defense)
"Ma, remember she's immature." My life was again changed
by love. My daughter and I have a very unique relationship. She's not only my best daughter, she's my very good
friend. I love you daughtering! You are the other greatest
part of me.

Hopefully you understand the point I'm trying to illustrate. I hope that you're now reminiscing about how your
life was changed by love. I Corinthians 15: *Howbeit that
was not first which is spiritual, but that which is natural; and
afterward that which is spiritual.* Paraphrasing it says "first
the natural and then the spiritual." If we feel that way about
our children, how much more did God feel about us.
Jeremiah 1: *Before I formed thee in the belly I knew thee; and
before thou camest forth out of the womb I sanctified thee and
ordained thee a prophet unto the nations.* This "knew" speaks
of intimacy. Our parents can't say that. If they'd known
how we'd turn out, while we were still in the womb,
well . . .

Ephesians 1: *In whom we have redemption through his
blood, the forgiveness of sins, according to the riches of his
grace.* The value of this scripture and what it's done for me
wasn't real until God saved me on October 12, 1997. I was
baptized in his name and received the precious gift of the
Holy Ghost, evidenced by my speaking in other tongues.
That was the beginning of my spiritual understanding of a
life changed by love. Jesus has saved me, raised me, and

blessed me with the knowledge of who he is. He's everything to me. I love him more than life itself and everyday I worship him for his awesome sacrifice.

I was reading about the prodigal son in Luke 15. The bible says that he came to himself and made the decision to arise and go to his father. The way to God is up. God showed me something about the word "arise." First of all there are 147 references to that word in the King James Version of the bible. Most of those references were spoken when God was providing direction(s) and instruction(s). Why did he use that word? He knew the natural mind wouldn't automatically receive what he was saying. Arise isn't only referring to your physical position. Most times it was referring to your mental position. God says in Isaiah 55: *For as the heavens are higher than the earth, so are my ways higher than your ways, and my thoughts than your thoughts.* Therefore we have to elevate our thinking to receive the things of God.

Here is what blessed me. The bible says his father saw him a great way off. That's it. When Jesus, my Saviour, was on the cross, he saw me a great way off. He saw you a great way off. He didn't die for himself; he died on that cross for the whole world. John 3: *For God sent not his Son into the world to condemn the world; but that the world through him might be saved.* He was showing love for those who didn't and wouldn't love him but even that didn't stop him. I'm reminded of the scripture in Hebrews 11: *These all died in faith, not having received the promises, but having seen them afar off and were persuaded of them and embraced them, and confessed that they were strangers and pilgrims on the earth.*

Those persons listed in the household of faith embraced him and his promises afar off.

What about you? Have you embraced him and all that he did and wants to do in, through and to you? I have and now I live for him. I'm 38 years late, but I'm here and I thank him. If I had died without knowing him, I would have lived an unfulfilled life. Hebrew 11 goes on to say: *And these all having obtained a good report through faith, received not the promise. God having provided some better thing for us, that they without us should not be made perfect.* Thank you Jesus for that better thing; unprecedented love provided for me. The knowledge and acceptance of that love has produced "A Life Changed By Love"

Father God,

My prayer for this reader is that they're willing to have their life changed by the manifestation of your love. Lord, I pray that this manifestation will produce that abundant life you died to give them.

In Jesus Name,
Amen

Chapter 3

My First Prayer

My mom, sister, and I were living with my Uncle Bobby, Aunt Glynes and their family in Hollis, Queens on Two Second Street. (That's what we called 202nd Street). We'd all go to the candy store before and after school. Almost everyday someone would take candy from that store. I'm still unable to say steal. I was a scaredy cat and would never take any candy. I knew that I'd be the one who'd get caught. However, since no one ever did, I decided to branch out and take some candy. Well, I got caught! The storeowner called the house and informed my family. The thought of going home terrified me and as I did so that terror heightened. On the way home I mentioned that I was going to confess. I was telling on everyone since I wasn't the only one that had ever taken candy. I was just the one who'd taken candy *today*. I knew that once that fact was known things would change. My cousin

Terry said, "Lynn, that's not right." You shouldn't tell on everybody else just because you've gotten caught. "Too bad," I said. "I'm not the only one getting a beating tonight." Misery does love company!

When I arrived home, I was told to go upstairs to my room and wait for Uncle Bobby to get home. That's an experience, sitting and waiting for a beating. It's very similar to lying in the labor room, looking at the clock, as you time your contractions. You're thinking "It's coming, it's coming." As I sat there, I was filled with anxiety, disbelief, and fear. I was still the only one in trouble. My confession didn't change a thing. I knew of God and that I needed help QUICK! I got down on my knees and prayed to God. I don't remember the words, but I'm sure that I prayed with a broken spirit and a contrite heart. Although my prayer was sincere, I still received a beating. Then I found out that my confession had changed something. I received another beating for being a tattletale. Psalm 119: *Before I was afflicted I went astray.* Isn't that the truth!

Recently I read Daniel 10: *Then said he unto me, Fear not, Daniel: for from the first day that thou didst set thine heart to understand, and to chasten thyself before thy God, thy words were heard, and I am come for thy words.* Although it was now over thirty years later that scripture really blessed me. I felt that God had heard me all those years ago, and had now come for my words. I still had to be accountable and deal with the consequences of my actions during those thirty years. Yet just knowing that God was with me made those consequences easier to bear. The Spirit just said that back then I was stealing candy, but now I'm stealing every moment I can to commune with my Saviour.

34

A few years later, my mom took my sister and I to her friend's house to tarry for the Holy Ghost. My sister and I didn't understand what we were doing or why we were doing it. We had never met this lady or heard about any Holy Ghost. I remember attempting to tarry and at the same time wondering when this experience would be over. Now that I'm older and have some understanding of the word of God, I can appreciate Proverbs 4: *Wisdom is the principal thing*; (let me interject that The Holy Ghost is the wisdom of God) *therefore get wisdom: and with all thy getting get understanding.*

God blessed me with wonderful parents, Alvin and Grace Charles. God is a wonder; he birthed me through a vessel named Grace after having made grace available for me. He knew I would need it. Grace is often referred to as God's unmerited favor. Many times God has taught me biblical principles through the use of acronyms. I have one for Grace:

G-od's R-edemption A-t C-hrist's E-xpense

What about you? Have you experienced his grace? If not, it's available even now. I thank God for a mom whose desire was to provide her girls with the power needed to live the life God wanted them to live. God needed me to recognize my unfailing need for him and his power operating in my life. Life had beaten me up, broken me down, chewed me up, and then spit me out. John 6: *When they were filled, he said unto his disciples, Gather up the fragments that remain, that nothing be lost.* I remember reading that and realizing how fragmented I was. Jesus said gather up the fragments so that nothing shall be lost. Glory to God! I again tarried for the Holy Ghost. This time, on October 12, 1997, I received it. Do you remember your first prayer or the first prayer God answered?

The best place to be is in the presence of the Lord! Have you done so already today? If not, put this book down and, get to your secret place and spend time with him. He wants you all to himself. Matthew 6: *But thou, when thou prayest, enter into thy closet, and when thou hast shut thy door, pray to thy Father which is in secret; and thy Father which seeth in secret shall reward thee openly.* Scripture says shut the door. He doesn't want any interruptions or visitors, just the two of you. He doesn't want others to view the intimacy he shares with you. He wants to tell you how much he loves you and to give you that love, acceptance, affection and self worth. You can only receive them in his presence. Guess what, after you've concluded your prayer and have come out that closet, he'll make sure that everyone knows that you've spent time with him. If you have already done so today remember you can never pray too much.

Father God,

I pray that this reader will commit to spending more time with you in prayer. I pray that you meet them there and that your presence completely fills them. I know that their prayer time(s) will be their best time(s).

In Jesus Name,
Amen

Chapter 4

The Counselor

M y parents divorced when we were young. I saw how painful that experience was for my mother. She lost her self-confidence. She never really recovered from it. In elementary school I never talked much therefore I was diagnosed an introvert. Webster defines introvert as: to turn inward; an introspective individual. I spent several years in a class for special students. I prefer to use the word special, however others used the word retarded. We'd eat lunch in our classroom. We were dismissed from school a half hour earlier than the other students. We also had to have weekly sessions with the school guidance counselor. I will never forget Mrs. Reznikoff. She had big red hair. She would ask me to share my innermost feelings. I didn't feel comfortable doing that therefore I didn't. I would just go to listen to her talk. Those sessions provided a temporary release from my special classmates.

She'd tell me how much better I'd feel if I opened up to her. I didn't feel that talking to her about my family situation would change anything. Her door read Guidance Counselor, not Marriage Counselor. Our sessions continued for close to two years. I'm sure she thought I was coo-coo for cocoa puffs. I thought that she was too. She should have realized her methods weren't working. I have to commend her diligence in trying to help me. One day, like the prodigal son, I came to myself. I looked around the room at my classmates and thought; I have got to get out of here. I asked my teacher, Mrs. Barille, if I could go to see Mrs. Reznikoff. She emphatically replied, "Yes." I'm sure she thought "Finally!"

I gathered my belongings and went to Mrs. Reznikoff's office. This was the first time that I'd requested to see her; she was very happy about my visit. I answered her questions. I told her enough for her to think that I'd made progress in the class and was now ready to rejoin the real world. That was my last day in that special class. I have to admit that I was apprehensive about returning to the real world; having lunch in the cafeteria and being dismissed with the rest of the school. Those that know me know that I've been talking ever since.

I am sharing this experience for several reasons. I told Mrs. Reznikoff just enough information to be released from the class. I still had unresolved issues. I thank God for the various Counselors, Psychiatrists, and Psychologists. Nevertheless, those professionals, having obtained an extensive education in order to be licensed, aren't equipped to deal with all the needs of the people. Most patients, like myself, aren't willing to allow them to get to the root of the problem. Mark 11: *And in the morning they saw the fig tree dried up from the roots.* Determining and dealing with the root of every issue is vitally important for mental, physical, and spiritual health.

I recently read a passage of scripture in Isaiah 9: *For unto us a child is born, unto us a son is given: and the government shall be upon his shoulder; and his name shall be called Wonderful, Counsellor, The mighty God, The everlasting Father, The Prince of Peace.* I beseech you brethren; never ever stop reading the word of God. God can show you something new each time. I have read that scripture many times. However I just realized that I missed something very important. I always read the passage as he shall be called. Now that's good by itself. For even now he is being called and he shall always be called.

What I missed was that it says: *his name shall be called.* Glory to God! His name, Jesus is Counsellor. Colossians 3: *And whatsoever ye do in word or deed, do all in the name of the Lord Jesus, giving thanks to God and the Father by him.* Why? That name has the ability to reclaim, redeem, release, restore, reveal, and revive thus making you free. Acts 3 speaks of the healing of the lame man at the gate called Beautiful. My God. He was at a beautiful place with an ugly condition. Some even have a beautiful face and an ugly disposition. Well I'll leave that alone. That portion of scripture goes on to say *who, seeing Peter and John about to go into the temple, asked an alms. And Peter, fastening his eyes upon him with John, said, Look on us. And he gave heed unto them, expecting to receive something of them. Then Peter said, Silver and gold have I none; but such as I have give I thee: In the name of Jesus Christ of Nazareth rise up and walk.*

And he took him by the right hand, and lifted him up: and immediately his feet and ankle bones received strength. And he leaping up stood, and walked, and entered with them into the temple, walking, and leaping, and praising God. Power is released when you call that name.

The text goes on to say that the people wondered how this man was healed. Acts 3: *And as the lame man which was healed held Peter and John, all the people ran together unto them in the porch that is called Solomon's, greatly wondering. And when Peter saw it, he answered unto the people, Ye men of Israel, why marvel ye at this? or why look ye so earnestly on us, as though by our own power or holiness we had made this man to walk? The God of Abraham, and of Isaac, and of Jacob, the God of our fathers, hath glorified his Son Jesus; whom ye delivered up, and denied him in the presence of Pilate, when he was determined to let him go. But ye denied the Holy One and the Just, and desired a murderer to be granted unto you; and killed the Prince of life, whom God hath raised from the dead; whereof we are witnesses. And his name, through faith in his name, hath made this man strong, whom ye see and know: yea, the faith which is by him hath given him this **perfect soundness in the presence of you all.***

That text is so meaty. The solvent for any problem is his name, Jesus, and faith in that name. I bolded that section of the verse because I realized that I was in that special class because I didn't have perfect soundness. I was soundless therefore they thought I was a fruitcake. Maybe that's why I don't like fruitcake. But God! Now because of his name and my faith in that name I too have perfect soundness. I believe perfect soundness to be wholeness. I love that *in the presence of you all.* Some folks didn't think I'd get out of that class and believe me they were looking. I have come out the closet (or in my case the class) in the presence of them all. Glory to God!

The world has a term "The One Stop Shop." In other words, you can get everything you need in one location. Well the same and even more applies to Jesus. He's the answer to every question; he's the solution to every problem. When a person or a situation makes you want to go there he empowers you to hold your piece, while providing you with his peace. His ability stretches far beyond this world. I then understood why I felt no confidence in Mrs. Reznikoff's ability. I'm not belittling her. She provided the limited help she could. However my issues, like others who try to find solace on the couch of Dr. Whoever, could only be solved and resolved by Jesus, whose name shall be called Counsellor. That's just one of the many offices he holds. Calling his name brings comfort, fulfillment, joy, peace, power and an inner feeling of satisfaction. I now realize that healing from Mrs. Reznikoff would've been good, but wholeness from Jesus is far better.

Father God,

My prayer for this reader is that they will bring ALL their cares and concerns to you. Lord, help them to realize that not only can you do it, but that if they have faith in you and in your name, you will do it for them.

In Jesus Name,
Amen

Chapter 5

They Are Covered

I 've touched on the circumstances surrounding my daughter's surgery. Prior to that surgery the devil tried to make me lose my mind. He kept telling me how horrible it would be for her and how much pain she would experience. I remember wishing that I had her Scoliosis. Wishing changed nothing. (That's a message all by itself). I think I'll write that again. Wishing Changed Nothing! It hadn't happened to me. Her struggles started in my womb. In the fifth month of my pregnancy, I began to hemorrhage. I then learned I had a placenta previa. We survived that and now she had to face this challenge. Why God? I asked that question hundreds of times.

Kaneeka never let that experience hinder her. She continued to excel in school. She won an academic scholarship to attend Jimmy Buffet's Sea Camp in the Florida Keys. I was so happy for her. She'd endured so much pain. That would be a wonderful experience. However, I knew she would be spending a lot of time on the beach. I was sure she wouldn't want anyone to see her scar. I voiced my concerned to her. She replied, "I don't care if they see my scar. Glory to God!

Her response blessed and encouraged me because I thought of my (life) scars, the majority of which resulted from bad decisions. Oftentimes I'd go out of my way to hide them. The thought of someone even knowing, God forbid seeing, was more than I could bear. The devil wasn't the only one that had me bound. I've found that my enemy was "in-a-me or inner-me." I'm now grateful for those scars. They prove that I've made some unwise decisions. If I decided to do those things again, I'd have visual reminders, which should help me "come to myself." This book testifies to the fact that I'm no longer hiding those things that scarred me. I'm allowing my mess to be my message. If my scars don't help anyone else, they'll always help me. I edited this chapter at about 7 O'clock A.M. on January 11, 2003. I went back to bed and got up again at 10 A.M. I then read my daily devotionals. Interestingly enough, A. J. Russell's, "God Calling", records on January 11, that "Life has hurt you. Only scarred lives can really save." Talk about confirmation. I rest my case.

I appreciated Kaneeka's attitude yet I was still concerned. I knew that she felt that way now, but would she still feel that way when she actually got there? I didn't want anyone to make her feel embarrassed or intimidated. The morning she left, I had an awesome time with God in prayer. I was praying that she'd be O.K. and that she'd keep that attitude after she arrived in Florida. God comforted me. I realized that although the scar is visible; those rods aren't.

They are covered and secure and as long as they stay in their place she will be fine. That's critical because if her rods were visible they'd also be vulnerable. They are keeping her back straight. I began to thank God for allowing me to understand that those rods couldn't and wouldn't be seen. At that point he said, "They are covered." Anytime God speaks into your spirit it's powerful. The rods, not the scar, needed the covering. That statement enriched me for more than one reason.

God showed me that my sins, like those rods, are covered. Psalm 85: *Thou hast forgiven the iniquity of thy people; thou hast covered all their sin.* Hebrew 10: *And their sins and iniquities will I remember no more.* Now even as I type this he's showing me all the things that are covered as long as I stay under the blood. I am assured of abundant life, joy and peace. My relationship with Jesus covers me from dangers seen and unseen. That doesn't mean that I won't go through anything or be sick. It means that even when I do or am, his peace and his presence will be with me. He has the ability and the willingness to make all things work together for my good!!! God's provision has covered our sin debt! Yes, they are covered!

Some companies only provide limited or liability coverage. That's partial coverage. You may incur out of pocket expenses. God's coverage is always full. Look over your life and see all the things that he's covered for you. I recommend jotting a few of them down. 1 Samuel 30: *And David was greatly distressed; for the people spake of stoning him, because the soul of all the people was grieved, every man for his sons and for his daughters: but David encouraged himself in the LORD his God.* David isn't the only one who has to encourage himself in the Lord. You may have to. Meditating on what God has done for YOU will encourage you. My testimony may bless you, but your testimony will keep you!

I was just thinking about the story of Adam and Eve in the Garden of Eden. In Genesis 3: *And the eyes of them both were opened, and they knew that they were naked; and they sewed fig leaves together, and made themselves aprons.* I heard Bishop Alfred Nickels say that Adam and Eve were the first tailor and seamstress. The scriptures go on to say: *And they heard the voice of the LORD God walking in the garden in the cool of the day: and Adam and his wife hid themselves from the presence of the LORD God amongst the trees of the garden. And the LORD God called unto Adam, and said unto him, Where art thou? And he said, I heard thy voice in the garden, and I was afraid, because I was naked; and I hid myself.* When man covers himself, he still feels naked. It speaks to the fact that man, even putting forth his best effort, can't cover himself enough to feel satisfied in that covering.

What's even more interesting is that in that same chapter it says: *"Unto Adam also and to his wife did the Lord God make coats of skins and clothed them.* God is a wonder; we mess up, and then try to cover up and yet God clothes us. That's right, man covered (and still felt naked) but God clothed! It doesn't take a Holy Ghost revelation to recognize the vast difference between being covered and being clothed. Have you ever had to sleep under a cover that was too small? If someone asked if you had cover you'd have to reply yes. You didn't mention that you had to sleep in the womb position. Having cover and feeling covered are two entirely different things.

46

God's ultimate coverage is best displayed by his death on the cross by the shedding of his blood for the remission of sin.

The death of Jesus demonstrates that God's wisdom eradicated sin and its penalties from our lives. Thank you Jesus.

Isaiah 1: *Come now, and let us reason together, saith the LORD: though your sins be as scarlet, they shall be as white as snow; though they be red like crimson, they shall be as wool.* How wonderful! The God of the universe wants to reason with us.

I Peter 1: *But with the precious blood of Christ, as of a lamb without blemish and without spot.*

I John 1: *But if we walk in the light, as he is in the light, we have fellowship one with another, and the blood of Jesus Christ his Son cleanseth us from all sin.*

God gave me an acronym for the word Blood:

B-ecause L-ove O-rdered O-ur D-eliverance
Jesus made us free!

Father God,

My prayer for this reader is that they'd realize that you desire to cover them in every area of their life. Lord, give them that understanding and the peace that accompanies it.

In Jesus Name,
Amen

Chapter 6

Can You See?

I have always had 20/20 vision. I've never needed glasses. My sister, my brother, and even my daughter wore glasses. Now there are contact lens. I always prided myself on being able to see. It wasn't until I was saved that I realized how blind I was. As I write this book about my life, changed by God's love, I have to be honest and declare that although I had physical sight, I was spiritually blind. Isaiah 9: *The people that walked in darkness have seen a great light: they that dwell in the land of the shadow of death, upon them hath the light shined.* Acts 9 depicts the Saul/Paul conversion. Paul's drastically changed life illustrates the power that a great light produces in a life. It takes a great light shone in darkness to bring God the great glory he deserves. Understand that darkness has nothing to do with the time of day. John 3: *And this is the condemnation, that light is come into the world, and men loved darkness rather than light, because their deeds were evil.* Darkness is the result of a life without God. Jesus said in John 9: *As long as I am in the world, I am the light of the world.*

Proverbs 12: *The way of a fool is right in his own eyes and* Proverbs 21: *Every way of a man is right in his own eyes.* Today many are operating by their own eyes or perception and not reality. In my foreword I mentioned that I'm not providing verses, just Chapters because it's very important to read the entire chapter. Romans 12: *And be not conformed to this world: but be ye transformed by the renewing of your mind, that ye may prove what is that good, and acceptable, and perfect, will of God.* This scripture is accurate. I recognize the value in having a renewed mind. It must be renewed in order to activate our spiritual eyesight. The number 1 precedes the number 2 for a reason. Romans 12: *I beseech you therefore, brethren, by the mercies of God, that ye present your bodies a living sacrifice, holy, acceptable unto God, which is your reasonable service.* Notice the scripture says "And" which means after you've done something else. There will be no transformed mind without the submission of your body. Are you conformed, therefore needing reform, or are you transformed?

My question to you is can you see? My next question is what do you see? My final question is if what you see is being interpreted by a renewed mind? These questions are vitally important if you want to have your life changed by God's love. Additionally, if the answer to any of these questions is no, are you willing to do what it would take to be able to see?

The word of God is a valuable treasure. God already knew most of us would be messed up and need to be fixed up, before we could walk in all he purposed for us. Therefore he has every provision available in the book called the bible.

II Corinthians 8: *For if there be first a willing mind, it is accepted according to that a man hath, and not according to that he hath not.* Are you willing? My desire for those reading this book is that they'll be able to see biblical truths more clearly.

Many things aren't what they appear to be. Your appearance may be altered and you can look anyway you'd like. You can change almost everything on your body. I was watching CSI the other night. A man had committed a double murder. As the story progressed it was proven that one of the murdered victims was actually a male, not a female. I had watched it and wasn't aware that the victim was actually Bruce and not Patty. However, that explained the rage expressed during the killings. My God, truth can be deadly.

Again, things aren't always as they appear. You thought he loved you, but you later found that to be a lie. They told you that the next promotion would be given to you. It was given to another employee. She said you'd be best friends forever. Now she's the best friend of the new girl in town. Most of our problems are the result of not clearly seeing what was right in front of us.

This is so interesting. I have been working on this book all day. I just started on this chapter and I turned on the television to watch a new episode of Touched By An Angel. It's about Monica's evil identical twin Monique. Monica was spending the day with, the newest angel, Gloria. They had gone to a restaurant to have lunch. Monique called the restaurant and asked to speak to Monica. The waitress informed Monica that she had a phone call and that the phone was in the back. Monica wondered who was calling her there. She went to the back of the restaurant to respond to her call. As she did so Monique appeared, dressed exactly like Monica, and told Gloria it was now time to leave. Gloria sensed that Monica seemed different but she went along with her. What am I saying? Even though things appear the same we need discernment to tell that they are indeed different.

Many times we think we are seeing everything when actually we aren't seeing anything. You need the Holy Ghost, the Comforter. John 14: *But the Comforter, which is the Holy Ghost, whom the Father will send in my name, he shall teach you all things, and bring all things to your remembrance, whatsoever I have said unto you.* John 16: *Howbeit when he, the Spirit of truth, is come, he will guide you into all truth.* His job is to guide you into all truth. You won't ever see without the one who knows all and is able to reveal it to you. There is a saying "lights on nobody home." A light is left burning when you're away from home for a period of time. That phrase also refers to an individual whose response or corresponding action indicates they didn't understand even though they appeared to. Many have eyes that appear to see and ears that seem to hear.

II Kings 6: *And Elisha prayed, and said, LORD, I pray thee, open his eyes that he may see. And the LORD opened the eyes of the young man; and he saw: and, behold, the mountain was full of horses and chariots of fire round about Elisha.* Psalm 119: *Open thou mine eyes, that I may behold wondrous things out of thy law.* Acts 26: *To open their eyes, and to turn them from darkness to light, and from the power of Satan unto God, that they may receive forgiveness of sins, and inheritance among them which are sanctified by faith that is in me.* All these passages refer to the opening of spiritual eyes.

At the end of Touched by An Angel I became aware of a subtle trick of the enemy. Gloria eventually realized that Monique wasn't Monica. Monique had set the stage for a potentially dangerous occurrence. Gloria then went to thwart her plan. When she arrived the assailant was already attacking the victim. She told the assailant to let the victim go. At first he didn't. Then she cried out "In the name of God" stop and he did so and ran away. I've checked using an online search engine and there are 57 biblical references to "in the name of God." Most say in the name of the Lord, the everlasting God, in the name of our God, in the name of the Lord Jesus Christ our God, in the name of the Lord your God, in the name of the Lord his God, in the name of the only begotten Son of God. However none say do anything "In the name of God." There's never a problem when you mention God. There are many gods in today's society. There is safety in saying God is good, or speaking of God. However the problem comes when you mention the name of Jesus.

The bible is very clear about the name, Jesus, which is above every name. Philippians 2: *That at the name of Jesus every knee should bow of things in heaven and things in earth, and things under the earth. And that every tongue should confess that Jesus Christ is Lord, to the glory of God the Father.*

Colossians 3: *Whatsoever ye do in word or deed, do all in the name of the Lord Jesus Christ, giving thanks to God and the Father by him.* Rev 3: *I know thy works: behold, I have set before thee an open door, and no man can shut it: for thou hast a little strength, and hast kept my word, and hast not denied my name.*

For the sake of ratings, television programmers don't want to offend viewers. Therefore they steer clear of the name Jesus. However, we should always stand for what we believe. Destiny's Child even had a song entitled, Say My Name. I believe that's what Jesus wants us to do. What am I saying? Physical eyesight is necessary. However discerning spiritual eyesight is even more necessary. Why? The reason is that spiritual, not physical, blindness will keep you from going to heaven.

There are two references that illustrate my point.

Matthew 20: *And, behold, two blind men sitting by the way side, when they heard that Jesus passed by, cried out, saying, Have mercy on us, O Lord, thou Son of David. And the multitude rebuked them, because they should hold their peace: but they cried the more, saying, Have mercy on us, O Lord, thou Son of David.* The scriptures identify that these two men were physically blind. However when they heard (Glory to God) that Jesus passed by, their actions showed that they saw more clearly than anyone around them. The reference to thou Son of David shows that they really knew who Jesus was. The spiritually blind in this passage of scripture were those who could see. But could they?

There is another illustration of this in Mark 10: *And they came to Jericho: and as he went out of Jericho with his disciples and a great number of people, blind Bartimaeus, the son of Timaeus, sat by the highway side begging. And when he heard that it was Jesus of Nazareth, he began to cry out, and say, Jesus, thou Son of David, have mercy on me. And many charged him that he should hold his peace: but he cried the more a great deal, Thou Son of David, have mercy on me. And Jesus stood still, and commanded him to be called. And they call the blind man, saying unto him, Be of good comfort, rise; he calleth thee.* There is an additional message here. II Corinthians 4: *We having the same spirit of faith, according as it is written, I believed, and therefore have I spoken; we also believe, and therefore speak.*

Don't ever let man shut you up or stop you when you're trying get to Jesus. Cry the more! Jesus will stand still and command that you be brought to him. Remember cry the more until you see the way that Jesus wants you to see. The only way to identify what Jesus would want is to utilize all that he's left for you. You have authority in his name, his shed blood, his written word and his Holy Ghost.

I'm blessed by a message preached by Elder Clarence Gordon. It was taken from John 12: *The same came therefore to Philip, which was of Bethsaida of Galilee, and desired him, saying, Sir, we would see Jesus.* His message was entitled "We would see Jesus." Yes, that's right. See Jesus; see him in all that you do. I promise that once you see him you'll be able to say like the songwriter whose lyrics identify the benefits of healthy spiritual eyesight.

I can see clearly now, the rain is gone. I can see all obstacles in my way, gone are the dark clouds that had me blind. It's gonna be a bright, bright sunshiny day!!!!!

You'll even feel that way when the sun isn't shining outside. It'll be bright and sunshiny in your spirit. My closing question, and I pray that you answer honestly. Are you now ready to see?

Father God,

I pray that this reader is willing to have their spiritual eyesight opened to see as, how, and what you want them to see. Lord, help them to realize that without your help they'll be unable to see the things that are right in front of them.

In Jesus Name,
Amen

Chapter 7

Pass The Praise

P rayer provides an awesome opportunity to commune with God. The thought that God avails himself to man is unbelievable. Prayer for me is PAT: P-raise, A-ppreciation and T-hanksgiving. Prayer is your opportunity to be honest (come clean) with God and to be cleansed by your confessions to God. The shedding of his blood permits us to come to him. Rev 1: *And from Jesus Christ, who is the faithful witness, and the first begotten of the dead, and the prince of the kings of the earth. Unto him that loved us and washed us from our sins in his own blood.* Thank you Jesus.

Most of the thoughts for the chapters in this book were derived from God in prayer. I spend a lot of time telling God how awesome he is, and praising him for who he is and more importantly who he is in my life. Paul best describes my feelings in Acts 17: *in him we live, move and have our being.* He is, always was, and always will be God, but for so long, I didn't give him first place in my life. I was sitting on my own throne with very little results. Why? If I'm on my throne then Jesus is on the cross. Conversely, when Jesus is on the throne (of my life) then I'm on the cross. Therefore I appreciate his allowing me to know him as intimately as I do now. However at this point I'm playing "Praise Catch-up" for all my lost time. I just had a thought about ketchup. Some flavor their food with it. It's even red. Glory! What am I saying? Let's flavor our lives the same way we flavor our food by applying the power of Praise Catch-Up, or the blood, to all that we do. Revelation 12: *And they overcame him by the blood of the Lamb, and by the word of their testimony; and they loved not their lives unto the death.* That word of their testimony tells of all the blood has done in their lives.

Jesus says in Revelation 3: *Behold I stand at the door and knock.* I am so grateful that he stood and didn't just stop by for a moment. The rest of that verse of scripture says, "*if any man hear my voice and open the door I will come in and sup with him.*" I thank him for providing me with the opportunity to hear him. 1 Kings 19: *And after the earthquake a fire; but the LORD was not in the fire: and after the fire a still small voice.* He speaks in a still small voice. Philippians 2: *For it is God which worketh in you both to will and do of his good pleasure.* I'd never imagined that God would visit me. When I finally realized that it had to be him I didn't immediately open the door. My heart breaks at the thought of him standing at the door waiting for me to let him in. I should have been waiting for him. He says I will come in. The wonderful thing is that he does so knowing what he's coming into. He's so worthy to be praised. All we have to do is open the door for him and he will come in. He doesn't wait for us to get it together because he knows there is no getting together without him. He says in Jeremiah 31: *Yea, I have loved thee with an everlasting love, therefore through lovingkindness have I drawn thee.* I am so grateful that his love is everlasting. People tend to love you for a period of time and if you aren't responsive during that time you may lose your chance for their love. God says my love is ever-lasting, so come when you are ready for me. He's always ready for you!

Many times in prayer I am so caught up in the praise. During one of those times I said, "Lord I know I need to pray for others but I can't seem to get pass the praise." That hit my spirit and thus provided this chapter title. God is worthy to be praised 24/7 so as far as he's concerned I don't ever have to get pass the praise. As I considered that phrase, I realized that it's two-fold. I've already identified the original thought. I've realized that God initiated Network Marketing. The intent of Network Marketing is to duplicate a proven, successful principle. Genesis 1: *be fruitful, multiply and replenish.* How do you pass the praise? You do so by living an obedient, visually effective, fruit-bearing life. This allows others to see that your lifestyle has resulted in a vibrant relationship with God. Then they want to duplicate your praise lifestyle to obtain their own dynamic relationship with God. Are you ready to pass the praise?

I watched a movie entitled Pay it Forward. I didn't understand what the title meant until I viewed the movie. Pay it Forward is a principle that says that you receive a blessing you don't deserve from someone you don't know. You are NOT to go back and bless that person. You become obligated to do the same by blessing someone you don't know who doesn't deserve it. It's a remarkable concept, which changed the hearts of the people in that town. Its effects were far reaching and produced wonderful results by all who cooperated with and operated by its dictates. That's what Jesus did for us. His death allowed us to receive a blessing that we didn't deserve from someone we didn't know. However what he did was much better, because in the movie they each did it for one person, he did it for the entire world.

The preaching of the gospel is an attempt, orchestrated by God, for man to Pass God's Praise in order to save souls. When preached by, and received with, the right heart the gospel is extremely effective in saving much people alive. The reality of God's word matures our spirit. Living a God-fearing life is an effective way to Pass God's Praise. Notice I didn't say living a godly life. That's because many who appear to live a godly life aren't God fearing. Psalm 111: *The fear of the LORD is the beginning of wisdom: a good understanding have all they that do his commandments: his praise endureth for ever.*

John 1: *He was in the world, and the world was made by him, and the world knew him not. He came unto his own and his own received him not. But as many as received him, to them gave he power to become the sons of God, even to them that believe on his name.*

1 John 3: *Behold, what manner of love the Father hath bestowed upon us, that we should be called the sons of God:*

therefore the world knoweth us not, because it knew him not. Beloved, now are we the sons of God, and it doth not yet appear what we shall be; but we know that, when he shall appear, we shall be like him; for we shall see him as he is.

The Son of God became the son of man; so that the sons of man could become the sons of God.

Father God,

My prayer for this reader is that they will also find it difficult to pass your praise. Lord, bless them with innovative ways to do so in order to lovingly affect this dying world.

In Jesus Name,
Amen

Chapter 8

It's a Heart Thing

The heart is vital to physical and spiritual health. The bible stresses the heart's importance in obtaining spiritual success. Deuteronomy 11: *And it shall come to pass, if ye shall hearken diligently unto my commandments which I command you this day, to love the Lord your God, and to serve him with all your heart and all your soul.* 1 Samuel 16: *But the Lord said unto Samuel, Look not on his countenance, or on the height of his stature: because I have refused him: for the Lord seeth not as man seeth, for man looketh on the outward appearance, but the Lord looketh on the heart.*

I Chronicles 29: *I know also my God, that thou triest the heart and hast pleasure in uprightness, As for me in the uprightness of my heart, I have willingly offered all these things.* Psalm 28: *The Lord is my strength and my shield, my heart trusted in him and I am helped.* Psalm 119 records four scriptures referring to seeking, observing, keeping thy precepts, and crying with the "whole heart." Another scripture in the same chapter says: *With my whole heart have I sought thee; O let me not wander from thy commandments.* God wants your whole heart. If he has your heart he has you. Proverbs 4: *Keep thy heart with all diligence, for out of it are the issues of life.* Matthew 12: *for out of the abundance of your heart, the mouth speaks.* Romans 10: *For with the heart man believeth unto righteousness.* Hebrews 10: *Let us draw near with a true heart in full assurance of faith.*

I recently watched a movie that really blessed me and solidified my understanding of the significance of a new heart. A detective, with a very rare blood type, needed a heart transplant. He was placed on a waiting list. The bible says in Jeremiah 17: *The heart is deceitful above all things and desperately wicked, who can know it? I the Lord search the heart.* God is actually waiting for us to desire that new heart. We are extremely blessed because we don't have to be placed on a waiting list for the new heart we need. The odds were working against this detective. The doctors felt that they'd be unable to locate a donor in enough time to save his life. However a woman was murdered and her blood type was compatible or worked. Ah yes, the blood works. Jesus' blood is compatible with every type. Romans 3: *Whom God hath set forth to be a propitiation through faith in his blood, to declare his righteousness for the remission of sins that are past, through the forbearance of God.* Romans 5: *Much more then, being now justified by his blood, we shall be saved from wrath through him.* Ephesians 2: *But now in Christ Jesus ye who sometimes were far off are made nigh by the blood of*

Christ. Hebrews 9: *And almost all things are by the law purged with blood; and without shedding of blood is no remission.* Have you been washed in his blood?

He received the heart of the murdered victim. This detective had solved many cases and had the reputation of being the best. This story was unique in that the donor's sister contacted this detective. She was aware of his reputation and wanted him to help solve her sister's murder. Normally a recipient knows nothing about the donor. However the victim's sister felt that the detective would feel an obligation to help her once he knew that he'd received her sister's heart. Like her sister's blood type, that worked. He told her that he would look into the case, but he wouldn't give any guarantees. Since he was now a heart transplant patient, he was on restricted duty. He also had to have weekly check-ups with his doctor.

The detective's life was drastically changed by the knowledge of the woman whose heart was now beating in his chest providing him life. As he studied her life he became more interested in finding out who murdered this beautiful young lady and left her son without a mother. He wasn't keeping his doctor appointments and began to look tired and run down. His doctor wanted to know what was going on. When he finally admitted what he'd found out about the donor, she was very upset and stated he wasn't supposed to know anything about her. She told him that although his heart was a gift he didn't owe the victims' family anything. His reply blessed me. He said, "A gift? She paid for this gift with her life." That sounds like Jesus. Glory to God! He went on to say that he WAS obligated to her. That's

right, because he was given a new heart; he felt an obligation to the owner of his heart. Ezekiel 11: *And I will give
them one heart and I will take the stony heart out of their flesh
and will give them a heart of flesh.* God gives us a new heart
without lengthy surgery and bodily scars. However we must
first be willing to cut some things out of our lives in order
to receive that new heart. Then he begins to do an inside
job. We, like the detective, should have (spiritual) check-
ups. A Christian must keep his heart saturated with the
word of God for proper spiritual operation.

The detective told his doctor that he would solve this
murder even at the risk of his own health. This is so good.
In other words, he would do whatever it took, even if it
killed him. If God has given you a new heart then you also
should be willing to do whatever it takes to live the life he
died to give you. DON'T LET HIS DEATH BE IN VAIN. At this point
in the movie, the victims' sister began to have feelings for
the detective. She was present during one of his examina-
tions. She then realized the detrimental physical toll this
investigation was having on him. His vitals were low and
his doctor was furious. The victims' sister requested he stop
his investigation. She was satisfied with knowing that he
had her sister's heart. She didn't want his health further
jeopardized by the stress of solving her sister's murder. Her
motives had changed because of her feelings for him. A
new heart will positively affect those around you. He replied that the case had given his life purpose and that it
was no longer just a case to him. Ezekiel 36: *A new heart
also will I give you, and a new spirit will I put within you; and
I will take away the stony heart out of your flesh and I will*

give you an heart of flesh. His new heart was working in and on him. I understood that. This is blessing me. Once you receive that new heart those things that once seemed irrelevant and meaningless to you now take on a new significant meaning.

He was diligent and solved the case. He was then asked what he would do with the rest of his life. His reply was the icing on this spiritually enlightening cake of a movie. He replied, "I have her heart and I'm willing to allow it to lead me." Glooooooory! That's it! We must be willing to allow that new heart of flesh to lead us. As I watched this movie I thought of the scripture in Luke 16: *And the lord commended the unjust steward, because he had done wisely: for the children of this world are in their generation wiser than the children of light.* This wasn't a religious movie and yet the spiritual implications were outstanding.

I found both those scriptures in Ezekiel interesting. It was the first time I had read anything positive about flesh. Biblical fleshly references are usually negative. Yet God says I will give you a heart of flesh. That heart of flesh allows you to receive the love and leadership of the Lord Jesus Christ. Ephesians 3: *That Christ may dwell in your hearts by faith; that ye being rooted and grounded in love.* Ephesians 6: *Not with eyeservice, as menpleasers; but as the servants of Christ, doing the will of God from the heart.* II Thessalonians 3: *And the Lord direct your hearts into the love of God, and into the patient waiting for Christ.* I Peter 3: *But sanctify the Lord God in your hearts; and be ready always to give an answer to every man that asketh you a reason of the hope that is in you with meekness and fear.*

That new heart and spirit provides the ability to operate as the above scriptures dictate.

I love word games. Let's discover how many words are within the word HEART: A, Art, At, Ate, Ear, Earth, Eat, Hat, He, Hear, Heat, Her, Rat, Rate, Tar, Tea, Tear, The. That's eighteen words. I hope you realize that if God placed all that within the five-letter word "Heart", he's placed even more within your beating heart. After all you are created in his image, after his likeness. II Corinthians 4: *For God, who commanded the light to shine out of darkness, hath shined in our hearts to give the light of the knowledge of the glory of God in the face of Jesus Christ. But we have this treasure in earthen vessels, that the excellency of the power may be of God, and not of us.* He's placed treasures in you and only a relationship with him can assist you in releasing them.

Now let's see how many sentences we can make from those eighteen words:

He hears.
He hears a tear.
He hears her.
He hears the earth.
He hears a rat
He hears the rat.
Hear (with) the ears (of your) heart
Her rat ate the tea.
His heart is in the earth.
Rate (what you) hear (by the word in your) heart.
The art (of a Christian is to) hear (with) the ears (of his) heart.

There are more like a rat ate; but I'll stop there.

It's A Heart Thing

Father God,

My prayer for this reader is that they'd be willing to allow you to give them that new heart of flesh. Lord, use that new heart to show them all the treasures you've hidden inside of them for the edifying of self and the body of Christ.

In Jesus Name,
Amen

Chapter 9

Give Up!

This term suggests surrendering. This is usually the state we're in when God gets us. We have finally gotten to the point where we realize that it's time for someone else to take the drivers seat in our life. God sighs and says FINALLY!!!!! John 3: *He must increase, but I must decrease.* Oh, the phone is ringing. I'll be right back. I'm back. God is a wonder. Eddie just informed me that there is a police chase going on in his neighborhood. He went on to say that the driver of the pursued car, obviously unaware, just drove onto a dead end street. Now it doesn't take Columbo, Matlock, or Perry Mason to figure out what happens next. He has run out of options. Here comes Officer Johnson to take him to jail. Talk about confirmation.

God usually gets us when we are busted, disgusted, down hearted, down trodden, helpless, hopeless, and sick and tired of being sick and tired. The interesting thing is that this is the place where he can do the best work on us and more importantly in us. Jonah 2: *And said, I cried by reason of mine affliction unto the LORD, and he heard me; out of the belly of hell cried I, and thou heardest my voice.* He's such a good God. Man doesn't want to have anything to do with us at this point, but God!

I am a single parent therefore I am accustomed to resolving my own problems. I had a 1987 Audi 5000. It began experiencing a car's slow death, however, I was unable to afford another vehicle. It frequently needed work. The bible says in Mark 16: *they shall lay hands on the sick, and they shall recover.* I laid hands on that car. It worked and I made it home without needing a tow truck. I took it to DP Imports on Wooster Pike. I was concerned about how much this repair would cost and couldn't wait for them to contact me. I called to find out what the problem was (this time). The response blessed me. The starter was off. That blessed my spirit. Glory to God! That phrase also summed up my entire life. Like my Audi, my starter had been off.

Proverbs 16: *There is a way that seemeth right unto a man; but the end thereof are the ways of death.* I laughed when I read this verse. I remembered that it seemed right to buy that dinette set from Elegant Junk. The store's name (wrong starter) should've been a clue. It didn't take long to realize that buying anything from Elegant Junk could only seem right. It was WRONG. Why? Junk, regardless of colorful surrounding terms, is still junk. I remember thinking that if I fall off this chair one more time I'll die. They wouldn't let me return it but they'd fix it when it broke. I only lived a few blocks away. They hadn't planned on that. I was there almost every other day. There's something about potential customers seeing previous customers coming in needing repairs on the junk they're considering buying. Eventually management mentioned that, because I lived so close, I could have my repairs done after hours. I thought about some other ideas that seemed right. I won't share those. Then I realized that I'd caused many of my problems by failing to give God the opportunity to have his will done in my life. I thank him for all the spiritual nuggets he's provided in the challenges of my life.

Jesus says in John 10: *No man taketh it from me, but I lay it down of myself. I have power to lay it down, and I have power to take it again.* What's the difference between laying down and being knocked or thrown down? Think about a vase. If I lay or place the vase down it will remain in tact. If the vase is thrown, grabbed, or even knocked down it will break. Choosing to lay your life down is far better than letting life beat you, knock you, or throw you down so hard that you never get up and graduate from the school of hard knocks. We tend to be more reactive than proactive. Matthew 21: *And whosoever shall fall on this stone shall be broken: but on whomsoever it shall fall, it will grind him to powder.* It's better to be proactive in your pursuit of God. When facing challenges we tell God that we'll surrender if he helps us resolve the problem. We say "I (WILL) Surrender All." When we're saying that, we have NO intention of surrendering at all. We really don't even want to surrender some. God wants complete control of EVERY area of your life. If he's not Lord of All, He's not Lord AT ALL! Give up and give in to the principles of God as dictated in the book called the bible. I guarantee that you'll never regret your decision.

Deuteronomy 30: *I call heaven and earth to record this day against you, that I have set before you life and death, blessing and cursing: therefore choose life, that both thou and thy seed may live."* Choose for yourself. Not making a decision is making a decision. However the outcome of that indecision is NOT one you can predict or control. Something is going to happen one way or the other. Give up!

I have an additional meaning regarding Give Up. Psalm 5: *My voice shalt thou hear in the morning, O LORD; in the morning will I direct my prayer unto thee and will look up.* God is above and kingdom living (heavenly principles operating in the earthly realm) demands that we look up and then give up to God those things that he deserves and desires. We look behind us, in front of us, to the right, and to the left without ever looking up for guidance. God wants us to allow him to have full reign in our lives. He wants us to be confident in him and in his ability to provide for us. Jesus says in Matthew 11: *Come unto me all ye that labor and are heavy laden and I will give you rest. Take my yoke upon you, and learn of me, for I am meek and lowly in heart: and ye shall find rest unto your souls.* Have you entered the rest of God? Just come and he'll give. We really are blessed to have a God that will do that for us!

Father God,

My prayers for this reader are that they'd feel a wrestling in their spirit and are now ready to give ALL up to you.

Give Up!

Lord, give them your power along with your peace as they do so.

In Jesus Name,
Amen

Chapter 10

Love God The Way He Deserves

The word love is abused and often misused. Those, who say they love you and yet do things that exhibit everything but love, break many hearts. Lives are cut short, people are incarcerated, and many live in their own man-made prison because of the misuse of this word love. Many are confused and have built internal walls to shield them from the pain often associated with love. Others, in despair, have sought comfort in all types of ungodly things because they felt that love wasn't worth it. Yet the bible says in I John 4: *He that loveth not knoweth not God; for God is love!!!* Many don't believe in God's love because what they thought to be love caused them pain.

The word of God is truth simply stated in John 17: *Sanctify them through they truth: thy word is truth.* So what happened? Many say they have love for you but they never get it around to you. What is your definition of love? That's the question that should be asked whenever that word is used. Your definition of love will determine how you feel about love. It also determines what you are willing to do and give for love. Love is many times determined by the value placed on the object of that love. We actually love a feeling, not the person providing that feeling. Unfortunately that love is temporary and conditional. As soon as the feeling is gone, so is the thought of love. The relationship then crumbles. That jilted person is left with many unanswered questions such as "I thought they loved me; how could this happen?" It is wise to clearly understand how the individuals involved define love before entering into a long-term relationship. We need to be very careful when using that word. The word love should be used in the context meant for its use.

We all have different ideas about what love is, what loves does and how love benefits us. Some, in hopes of receiving prestige, and even sexual favors, often give worldly illustrations of love. The value you place, whether real or perceived, on what that love connection will do for you will determine the extent of your willingness to love and the ways you'll express that love. Often times we have high expectations based on false information. This is illustrated in the book of Genesis, the 29th & 30th Chapter, in the story about Rachel, Leah and Jacob. *And he went in also unto Rachel, and he loved also Rachel more than Leah.* Later Leah began to have children for Jacob. *And Leah said, God hath endued me with a good dowry; now will my husband dwell with me, because I have born him six sons: and she called his name Zebulun.* However the bible had earlier identified that

Jacob loved Rachel more than Leah. Still, Leah felt that Jacob would love her and want to stay with her because of the sons she bore.

Many love certain foods, designer clothes, new cars and nice homes. The word love is a term of endearment meant to describe emotional feelings for people and/or pets, not to describe feelings for objects or things. Some love because of what was done for them or on their behalf. The value of what was done determines the depth of the love they feel and the actions they display because of that love. Although love should come from the heart often times it comes from the head. The bible says in Luke 7: *Wherefore I say unto thee, Her sins, which are many, are forgiven; for she loved much but to whom little is forgiven, the same loveth little.* So accordingly, I'd paraphrase by stating that whosoever has been forgiven much loveth much. That is very true. When you realize that you didn't deserve what was given to or for you, that realization makes you experience the benefits of love.

In other words, you are the rescued who loves the rescuer. Colossians 1: *Giving thanks unto the Father, which hath made us meet to be partakers of the inheritance of the saints in light. Who hath delivered us from the power of darkness, and hath translated us in to the kingdom of his dear Son (Jesus). In whom we have redemption through his blood, even the forgiveness of sins. Who is the image of the invisible God, the firstborn of every creature.* This is exactly why we all should be crazy about Jesus. Yes I mean crazy. A crazy person is subject to do just about anything. Likewise, if you are crazy about Jesus, you should be willing to do anything and everything he says in the Holy Bible. Kelli Williams has a song on her "IN THE MYX (OF YOUR WILL)" Gospel CD entitled "CRAZY FOR U." The lyrics are as follows:

Floating around in a daze, Jesus your love is amazing, amazing. A debt I cannot repay. Oh, what a change in my life you have made. I'm just cra-zy, cra-zy for you Jesus. I can't help it, there's just something about the way, the way you love me. People just don't understand when, I tell them I've got a man, got a man. But it's a man they can't see, someone who cares about me, about me. Like a clown in the circus, I'm just crazy for your loving Jesus. Some body better turn me in, cause I'm getting crazier by the minute. Heads going around in circles Jesus, all I really want to do is please you. I'll tell the whole world that I need you. Crazy Faith, I trust and believe you.

Glory (that's me) not Kelli. Hold on, I'll be right back. I'm going to listen to it now. I had to listen to that song twice.

We've discussed what love isn't, now let's define what it is. Love is an action word. Love manifests by doing. The bible is a love story. Genesis through Revelation speaks about God's love and provision for those who didn't deserve it. Yet he gave it anyway. Romans 5: *But God commendeth his love toward us, in that, while we were yet sinners, Christ died for us.* 1 Corinthians 13 gives an awesome definition of love. It's much better than Webster's definition. I want to illustrate something for you. In some instances, the bible defines love as charity.

Let's replace charity with love:

Love suffereth long and is kind.
Love envieth not.
Love vaunteth not itself, is not puffed up.
Love doth not behave himself unseemly, seeketh not his own and is not easily provoked, thinketh no evil.
Love rejoiceth not in iniquity, but rejoiceth in the truth.
Love beareth all things, believeth all things, hopeth all things, endureth all things.
Love never fails.

Now let's replace love with God:

God suffereth long and is kind.
God envieth not.
God vaunteth not itself, is not puffed up.
God doth not behave himself unseemly, seeketh not his own and is not easily provoked, thinketh no evil.
God rejoiceth not in iniquity, but rejoiceth in the truth.
God beareth all things, believeth all things, hopeth all things, endureth all things.
God never fails.

If you have read the bible then you must realize that all the above verses are true about the character of God. It has to be true because God is love!!!!! Therefore I conclude that God's love is active. His love is best demonstrated by the death of Jesus on the cross. 1 John 4: *In this was manifested the love of God toward us, because that God sent his only begotten Son into the world, that we might live through him.* His love cares, comforts, covers, creates, decides, edifies, gives, lifts, manifests, participates, plants, prefers others, provides, provokes, and always thinks the best. I'm sure that there are other action words to describe his love. Now let's look at the love of God. *Abraham said, "God will provide himself . . ."* God provided himself then and is still doing so even now.

We recently embarked on an expansion at our church. The new edifice is remarkable. I thank God for enlarging our territory. We now have room for the many souls he will send. We recently held a Grand Opening for the surrounding businesses. Bishop Bowers, affectionately known as "The Preaching Machine", now enjoys a fine new office. I spoke with him during the Grand Opening and casually mentioned that I had heard about how beautiful his office was. His eyes lit up and he proceeded to give me a personal tour of his office. His office is regal, spacious, and beautifully decorated. Bishop has been preaching Jesus for close to fifty years. As I stood in his office all I could say over and over again was "Bishop, you deserve this." I walked away from that tour feeling really good about what I'd seen and even special because he'd taken the time to give me a personal tour. After all, he's the Bishop.

I was telling Sister Washington that I had just seen Bishop's office. She mentioned that he'd given her a personal tour. I had to smile. I thought he's just like Jesus in that he also has the ability to make everyone feel special. I considered my response regarding Bishop's deserving that office. I thought: if Bishop deserved that because of his faithfulness, how much more does Jesus deserve?

My challenge to you was to love him the way he deserves to be loved. However I must apologize to you: for I now realize that mankind isn't capable of loving God the way he deserves to be loved. Therefore my challenge has been redefined. Let's look at what he's done. He blessed, empowered, lifted, loved, raised, and saved you. He's provided goodness, grace, loving kindness, and mercy to and on your behalf. He's promised to never leave or forsake you. He sent the Holy Ghost to be our abiding comforter. Therefore my new challenge is this, TO THE VERY BEST OF YOUR ABILITY, love him like he deserves to be loved! You must understand that even in putting forth your best ability, he still won't be loved like he deserves. However I encourage you to give it all you've got! Let me give you some direction in doing so. Think of new ways to let him know, through your lifestyle, how much he means to you. Obedience to ALL of the word of God is the best way to demonstrate your love for God.

Father God,

I pray that this reader will become willing, through their love for you, to become broken break and poured out wine: so that the sweet smelling savor of their broken alabaster box will send your presence into the lives of all they come in contact with.

In Jesus Name,
Amen

Debt Free

I am so thankful to God for all the spiritual lessons he's taught me through the understanding of natural things. Before I begin to share my story, I need you to understand that I am explaining not complaining. There is only a thin line between them. You see, too much explaining can lead to complaining; but I promise I won't go there. I'm just illustrating a point.

I am a single parent, with two children, and have always struggled financially. I moved to Cincinnati from New York. I had already accumulated credit card debt and since I still had a few cards left, I acquired more. My credit card debt was a result of need, not of greed. I had to use credit to pay bills that I didn't make enough money to pay. I had mastered the credit card game. No pun intended. I knew that you never reduce the principle if you only send the minimum payment. I would always send the minimum payment plus the finance charge. That reduces the principle. I was sent applications for new cards with low introductory rates. Once I received the card, I'd note that rates expiration date in my planner. A month before the expiration date, I'd contact other lenders in an attempt to obtain a lower rate from them. If so, I'd transfer the balance to that lender before the introductory rate expired. The benefit of transferring balances is that the transferred balance counts as a payment. I wouldn't have to make a payment that month. I played that game and played it well. After God saved me, I recognized that the book called the bible says in John 8: *If the Son therefore shall make you free, ye shall be free indeed.* That scripture is often misquoted. Many say "whom the son sets free is free indeed." There is a big difference between being set free and being made free. It takes much more effort to be made free. Jesus paid the ultimate price with his life.

Some of us have to go around and around the same mountain before we get it. Deuteronomy 1: (*There are eleven days journey from Horeb by the way of mount Seir unto Kadesh-barnea). And it came to pass in the fortieth year in the eleventh month, on the first day of the month, that Moses spake unto the children of Israel, according unto all the LORD had given him in commandment unto them.* That chapter goes on to say: *The Lord our God spake unto us in Horeb, saying Ye have dwelt long enough in this mount.* When you're set free you have the same mindset. Therefore (eventually) you'll do what you've always done. However, when you're made free your experiences have changed your mindset. A changed mind changes its actions. Psalm 119: *It is good that I have been afflicted, that I might learn thy statutes.* When you go through something, get something out of it by learning life's lesson. Go through, to get to: so that you won't have to go around that same mountain again. Actually don't just go through, grow through. I don't know about you, but I've decided that I don't have another forty years to spend on an eleven-day trip.

Ephesians 4: *But speaking the truth in love may grow up into him in all things, which is the head, even Christ.* I just thought of another misquoted scripture. Ephesians 3: *Now unto him that is able to do exceeding abundantly above all that we ask or think, according to the power that worketh in us.* Most say exceedingly abundantly. That's probably due to the excitement that arises when you understand the significance of the verse. However, exceeding is good all by it self. It needs no—ly. I lovingly challenge all who read this book, and have misquoted those scriptures in the past, to be mindful to quote them correctly.

Let me get back to my thought. Debt is bondage and I wanted and needed to be free. I'd memorized all the prosperity scriptures and was fervent in my declaration of God's word to God. The bible says in Galatians 4: *But it is good to be zealously affected always in a good thing.* I was really excited when I read 3rd John: *Beloved I wish above all things that you'd be in health and prosper, even as your soul prospers.* After all, I was growing in my knowledge of the word and maturing in my Christian walk. I was weeping and wailing out to God almost every day. "God, show me what to do to be debt free!" "Please God, Please." This went on for what seems an eternity.

I'm thankful that God knows my heart. My heartfelt desire was to walk in the freedom he had ordained for me.

I guess I was going overboard. One day I heard the Holy Ghost say "You are debt free, stop begging for what you already have." At first I didn't understand that response. Although there are a few suddenly's and a few straight a ways in the bible, most people had to wait for the manifestation of the things they believed God for. I believed God and was anticipating that manifestation. I didn't know how and didn't know when but I believed that I was debt free. Every day I looked for a check in my mailbox. Finally a check came. I was so excited. I could hardly open the envelope. Well once I did, I could hardly believe it. The check was for $2.50. I had been sure that God knew the right amount. I stopped begging for a season.

After a few more months and no manifestation, I went back to God and said "God, I thought you said that I was debt free." Then I received a response that changed my attitude forever. The response came in the form of the following question. "Would you rather have financial freedom and responsibility for the consequences of your sins, or be free from the ramifications of sin and be financially challenged?" Immediately I understood that where it mattered the most, I was debt free. I could stand before Jesus being justified and made right because he was the propitiation for all sin.

Propitiation is a profound word. Men of Standard sing a song and the lyrics give a good definition of this word. The lyrics are *"after all the wrong I've done, you're the only one who can forgive me and bring me back to you."* They have to be singing about Jesus. Oftentimes you may be forgiven but you're never put back in your original state. Look at

God. It's one thing to be restored in your relationship with man; it's far better to be restored to and in God. We've all heard about Humpty Dumpty. He sat on a wall and had a great fall. Let me interject that pride puts you up and then ultimately causes you to fall. All the kings' horses and all the kings' men couldn't put Humpty together again. Therein lies the problem. They sought the kings' horses and his men without seeking the King himself. Jesus was the only one who could restore our fallen state by shedding his blood.

I wouldn't have been able to stand in God's presence with my sins. Now I knew, I was debt free. My sin debt was paid in full. Glory!!!!! So guess what happened or should I say what didn't happen? I have never prayed that debt free prayer again. I know the bible says in John 8: *If the Son therefore shall make you free ye shall be free indeed.* I also understand that a deed is paper and that could mean that God wants me to be free on paper. Don't misunderstand and think I'm saying that we have to be financially challenged to be in God. I'm not saying that at all. What I am saying is that I didn't supernaturally get in debt and that I shouldn't expect to be supernaturally delivered from debt; I now pray for God to give me the wisdom to handle my finances in a way that will lead to financial freedom. I know that being baptized in Jesus name and receiving the gift of the Holy Ghost (with the evidence of speaking in tongues) has made me debt free; and for that I am blessed, grateful, and thankful. My sin debt far outweighed my financial debt.

I'm going to a place prepared for me called Heaven
Heaven is where I'm gonna spend eternity for ever
There'll be no crying; there'll be no dying in Heaven
Sickness will be no more; we'll sing and shout forever
in Heaven
When we all get to Heaven; What a day of rejoicing
that will be
When we all see Jesus, we'll sing and shout the
victory
Heaven
Tarralyn Ramsey

Thank you Jesus for making me debt free!

Father God,

My prayer for this reader is that they'd experience being made free. Lord, if they are financially challenged, help them to allow you to disperse the little they feel they have. Lord, I thank you for your ability to do so much with so little.

In Jesus Name,
Amen

Chapter 12

Social Security?

I love communing with the Lord. I've found a peace in his presence that I'd never experienced in all the other ways I had sought to find peace. I heard Mother Queen Esther Nickles say, "Come clean or stay away dirty." How insightful and accurate. God want us to share our cares and concerns with him. I have become comfortably accustomed to doing so. I appreciate the fact that I can share my innermost feeling with him.

My ex-husband was killed and for a period of time I received Social Security benefits. Those benefits were recently terminated. At first I began to wonder how I would meet my financial obligations. I expressed those concerns to God. I then realized that God, and not those benefits, allowed me to meet ALL my obligations. I began to repent to God and to thank him for the period of time that I had received Social Security benefits. During that prayer time the Lord revealed a relevant attitude.

It started when I said "thank you for my Social Security benefits." That really spoke to my spirit. I thought Social Security benefits. I began to realize that many times we seek the benefits that come from the company we keep. The world gives certain benefits depending on who you are or whom you're related to. Others love to name drop to receive certain privileges. Oftentimes the familiar is what hinders us from securing a relationship with God.

Let's look at an example. Genesis 12: *Now the Lord said unto Abram, get thee out of thy country and from thy kindred, and from they father's house unto a land that I will shew thee: And I will make of thee a great nation, and I will bless thee, and make they name great; and thou shalt be a blessing; And I will bless them that bless thee, and curse him that curseth thee; and in thee shall all families of the earth be blessed.* The Lord instructed him to get away from the familiar. *So Abram departed, as the LORD had spoken unto him; and Lot went with him; and Abram was seventy and five years old when he departed out of Haran.* Notice that the Lord had told Abram to get away from his kindred yet scripture goes on to say that Lot went with him. Social Security?

Genesis 13: *And Lot also, which went with Abram had flocks, and herds, and tents. And the land was not able to bear them, that they might dwell together; for their substance was great, so that they could not dwell together.* Well, isn't that something. Things never work out when we go against God's wishes. God knows how to end a relationship. That chapter goes on to say *And the Lord said unto Abram after that Lot was separated from him.* Many times God can't even speak with us until we get away from the familiar.

II Kings 5: *But Gehazi, the servant of Elisha the man of God said, Behold my master hath spared Naaman this Syrian, in not receiving at his hands that which he brought; but, as the LORD liveth, I will run after him and take somewhat of him.* The bible goes on to record that Gehazi followed after Naaman, lied and stated that the gift was for two young men of the sons of the prophets. He used his social security to obtain benefits by capitalizing on his association with Elisha. Gehazi obtained two talents of silver in two bags, with two changes of garments. However when questioned he lied to Elisha and told him that *"thy servant went no whither."* Elisha knew what Gehazi had done. Therefore the leprosy of Naaman cleaved to Gehazi and would be to his seed forever. What am I saying? Make sure that you really know those that are closest to you. Some may only want the benefits of being associated with you.

Jesus says in Luke 14: *If any man come to me, and hate not his father, and* mother, *and wife, and children, and brethren, and sisters, yea, and his own life also, he cannot be my disciple.* The severing of these family ties will cause a lot of pain. However we must still possess a "Thankful" attitude towards God.

I've had sickness and I've had pain
My heart has been broken and my life has been strained
But in spite of everything I've been through, I still gotta
say Thank You.
I've been up and I've been down; had my life turned
completely around. But in spite of everything I've been
through, I've still gotta say, Thank YOu!
Still Say, Thank You
Smokie Norful

God wanted me to clearly understand that those Social Security benefits and everything else that's not of, through, and in him are also temporary. Matthew 24: *Heaven and earth pass away, but my words shall not pass away.* God wants us to feel content with and complete in him. Colossians 2: *And ye are complete in him, which is the head of all principality and power.*

Father God,

My prayer for this reader is that they'd recognize that everything comes from you. Lord, give them the strength to end all ungodly relationships regardless of their chances of being alone.

In Jesus Name,
Amen

Chapter 13

School Daze

I attended Andrew Jackson High School in Queens, N.Y. and graduated in June 1977. It's hard to believe that's almost 26 years ago. During those years, I've gone through a lot of experiences, both good and bad. Life presents a combination of both. I hope that your good experiences exceeded your bad ones. Let me encourage those who've experienced more bad than good. It's not over, you can ensure that your latter be better than your former. Are you ready?

The majority of those years I was a single parent. Those years were challenging, stressful and I even experienced some trauma. I heard Bishop Noel Jones call stress and trauma "STRAUMA". I like that. I was blessed in that my son is six years older than my daughter. He was my live in babysitter. I sometimes had to work as many as 12–14 hours a day. Many times I left one job and went directly to the other one. It's good to be faithful to your present day call. My call, during those years, was to raise my children and provide them with a stable home life. God's word details instructions on raising and being responsible to and for them. They didn't have everything but I'm confident that they knew they were loved.

You didn't know that you'd be raising your child on your own. You're still obligated to be the best parent you can be. My understanding of the reality of my situation helped me accept the decisions I had to make. I had to put first things first. In 1988, I read about a correspondence course taken via the mail. I enrolled in an Accounting class. I had to meet weekly and monthly deadlines. I maintained an "A" average and received a certificate of completion. Still, the fact that I never attended college sometimes bothered me. When I felt bothered I reminded myself of my present day calling.

Then, there was the threat of unemployment on my job. I realized that you never get a second chance to make a first impression. Unless you are seeking employment with some-one you know, your resume is your first impression. I wasn't confident about that first impression. Why would some-one choose me over another candidate with a college degree? Although I was eventually blessed with another position, that concern lingered. The company I worked for paid 100% tuition up front. However, I didn't want to go to college at night.

Tony graduated from Tennessee State University in May 2000. His friend, Cool Mill, had obtained a lucrative position working with computers. The last week in August, during one of our conversations, he said "Ma; if you go to school you should go for computers." I felt that under the right circumstances, I would commit to obtaining an Associate Degree.

The first Sunday in September, I was reading the paper. A brochure about Antonelli College, located on Seventh Street downtown, was enclosed. I wasn't aware that there was a college downtown. Luke 14: *For which of you, intending to build a tower, sitteth not down first, and counteth the cost, whether he have sufficient to finish it.* Antonelli, offered an Associate Degree Program in Computers, and was four blocks from my place of employment. I thought "If I went to Antonelli, I'd graduate being smart and slim." What a great combination. That college was already beneficial and I wasn't even enrolled yet. I contacted the school and met with the counselor. He stated that if I began on September 25, 2000, I would graduate in June 2002.

My employer approved my request for tuition and adjusted my work schedule. Thereby allowing me to go to school full-time during the day and work twenty-one hours a week. I was scheduled to attend classes on that Monday morning. God was doing this thing. He used my son to direct my path. I knew that eventually Tony would say something that I'd be willing to take heed too.

God reminded me of something. My father, Alvin Charles, had a Federal job as a United States Customs Inspector. One night, approximately thirty years ago, he came into our room and informed my sister and I that he was going back to school. We looked at each other and I replied, "Daddy that's nice." *Wisdom is the principal thing.* After he left the room we snickered that Daddy was crazy. Needless to say he went. Well guess what? I'm pretty sure that my father and I were the same age when we returned to school. My dad was my forerunner.

Times have changed and now it's not unusual to see all ages in the college classroom. I had always been smart in school but again that was 25 years ago. I was apprehensive but also exhilarated because I would finally be able to attend college and obtain a degree. The blessing for me was that I was now saved and diligently trying to be led by the Spirit of God. That is key for whatever we do. I remember praying and thanking God for this opportunity and asking him to go with me everyday and in everyway. I can say like TLC, that when it comes to God, I ain't too proud to beg. In doing so, I've learned that in God WAILING WOMEN WIN!

Although I was now a mature adult, I begged the Lord not to send me to school without him. God not only showed up with me, but he also showed out in me. He allowed me to see spiritual principles in every class. The first one occurred in my computer class when the instructor stated that the program wasn't case sensitive. You could use upper or lowercase letters and obtain the same result. As tears fell from my eyes I thought, I am so grateful that Jesus is not case sensitive. My case is different from your case. My Pastor Bishop Paul A. Bowers said it best, "before you ever knew there was a case; Jesus was already on the case." Thank you Jesus!

I had to take Microsoft PowerPoint, Word, Access, and Excel. The Lord told me that you must know your Power point, (which is Jesus). You only know that through the

Word. That knowledge provides Access and because of that access, you will Excel. I learned about the AIDA concept in my Marketing Class. The AIDA concept outlines the process for achieving promotional goals in terms of stages of consumer involvement. AIDA is an acronym for Attention, Interest, Desire and Action. Wow, that is surely spiritual. God, using varied methods, gets our Attention, draws our Interest to him, and Desires that we know him, that knowledge challenges us to take Action for him.

My Public Speaking class taught us The Art of Public Speaking. How important because delivery impacts discovery. Oftentimes it's not what you say, it's how you say what you say. John 4: *And many of the Samaritans of that city believed on him for the saying of the woman, which testified, He told me all that ever I did. So when the Samaritans were come unto him, they besought him that he would tarry with them: and he abode there two days. And many more believed because of his own word. And said unto the woman, Now we believe, not because of thy saying, for we have heard him ourselves, and know that this is indeed the Christ, the Saviour of the world.*

The class concentrated on giving speeches and identifying the different types of speeches. We learned about credibility. Credibility is the audience's perception of whether a speaker is qualified to speak on a given topic. There are two major factors influencing a speaker's credibility. They are competence and character. Competence is how an audience regards a speaker's intelligence, expertise or knowledge on the subject. Character is how an audience regards a speaker's sincerity, trustworthiness and concern for the well being of the audience. The different types of credibility are initial, derived and terminal. Then there is the Speech Communication Process, which includes: Speaker, Message, Channel, Listener, Feedback, Interference and Situation. These elements affect the response to the message.

The speaker: The person who is presenting an oral message to the listener.

The message: Whatever a speaker communicates to someone else.

The channel: The means by which a message is communicated.

The listener: The person who received the speaker's message.

The feedback: The messages, usually nonverbal, sent from a listener to a speaker.

Interference: Anything impeding the communication of a message. Interference can be external or internal to listeners.

Situation: The time and place in which the speech communication occurs.

Let's look at this from a spiritual prospective. This speech communication process illustrates the steps to preaching the gospel of Jesus Christ and how important credibility is in receiving Salvation.

The speaker: The preacher/teacher/witness.

The message: The gospel, obtained only from the Word of God.

The channel: The pulpit, television, radio conversation etc.

The listener: Are they receptive? Are they listening to the spirit or to the speaker?

The feedback: Is there a positive verbal or non-verbal response to the message?

Interference: A closed mind, distractive audience, busyness.

The situation: This is critical to God. Time and place must be conducive for us to receive from God.

In my Communications class, I learned about The Five C's of good writing and their application to business writing. They are:

Conciseness: Writing (Speaking) the message in as few words as possible.

Completeness: Ensuring that all information needed by the reader (hearer) to respond or act is included.

Courtesy: Showing consideration for the reader (hearer).

Clarity: Writing (Speaking) Clearly.

Correctness: Accuracy of all statements and details.

Not only are these principles effective and applicable to business writing, but also for preaching, teaching and witnessing the Word of God.

I submit that there are also Five C's, which identify necessary steps in completing what God has purposed for your life. Those five C's are listed below:

Call: Hearing the Voice of God.

Challenge: The ability to overcome circumstances that threaten and always accompany the call.

Comfort: The sustaining peace of God given to encourage you on your journey.

Choice: Making a decision to finish your course with joy. *Godliness with contentment is great gain.*

Celebrate: This is your reward for what you allowed God to do to you, with you and ultimately through you.

My concentration in college was Network Administration. Dennis Maione, MCT, authored MCSE Windows 2000 Server Training Guide. This book has approximately eight hundred pages. When I first received that book I thought; "this is just too much book for me." However, I glanced at the Table of Contents and the Spirit led me to read the authors dedication of the book. Most dedications mention those that played a major part in the completion of the book. The last sentence of this dedication blessed me and at that point I was better equipped to tackle the material in the book. I have never read a textbook dedication like this before. It reads as follows:

> Finally, to anyone else I know and love (fill in your name here) thank you for your patience with me as I grow up into the image of Jesus.
> Thank you, Dennis.

God is a wonder. He knew my concern as I considered the contents of the book. God always confirms his presence with us. A server is a computer and software that receives request(s) from client computers (that are connected to it) and then shares it's resources (data) with that client computer. The result is a client/server relationship. The server is configured to store programs and data which is to be used by the client computers. Oh My God! In the natural, a server's job is to provide for, give to, wait on, attend to, help, promote, advance and distribute. Oftentimes most of this provision is done in advance since the server has already anticipated the most important needs of the client.

Jesus is our best example of a server. He hears the requests of those that are connected to him. He has one over the natural server; for he can even hear requests from those that aren't connected at the time they request resources. Glory to God! He has the ability to meet every need and best of all he is willing to do so. He has been providing himself from the very beginning. Isaiah 7: *Therefore the Lord himself shall give you a sign, Behold a virgin shall conceive and bear a son, and shall call his name Immanuel. Isaiah 9: For unto us a child is born, unto us a son is given, and the government shall be upon his shoulder.* In Mathew 1: *And she shall bring forth a son and thou shalt call his name JESUS for he shall save his people from their sins.* Later on, in the same chapter, it reads" *Behold a virgin shall be with child and shall bring forth a son, and they shall call his name Emmanuel, which being interpreted is, God with us.* Finally John 1: *And looking upon Jesus as he walketh, he saith Behold the Lamb of God!* Truly Mary had a little lamb, whose fleece was white as snow.

In the computer world Ram, Random Access Memory, stores data. However in the spiritual realm, Ram is an acronym for:

Revelation without Application produces no Manifestation

I considered the title I'd give to my reference to college. School Daze is very applicable. Daze, referencing days, and the many times I dazed out the window thinking about how great God is.

*Floating around in a daze, Jesus your love is amaz-
ing, amazing, a debt I could not repay, Oh! What a
change in my life you have made.*

**Excerpt from the Kelli Williams Gospel CD
In the MYX (OF YOUR WILL)**

My final thought is taken from my Psychology class. I
would purchase my textbooks online because I could save
on the cost. However, to order online, I needed the textbook title, author, and ISBN number. The book I used in
that class was authored by Gerald and Marianne Schneider
Corey and entitled "I NEVER KNEW I HAD A CHOICE."
Glory to God! I'm writing to tell you that you have a choice
and to encourage you to heighten your awareness of your
available choices. Choices like deciding if the cup is half
full or half empty, like deciding to be bitter or better, like
deciding whether you'll continue to let your past determine your future. Deuteronomy 30:*I call heaven and earth
to record this day against you, that I have set before you life
and death, blessing and cursing: choose life, that both thou
and thy seed may live.* We serve a God that allows us to
make our own choices and decide the type of life we wish
to live. Jesus said in John 10: *"I am come that you might
have life and have it more abundantly.* He offers two choices,
life and a better life. Bless you Jesus.

My daughter Kaneeka and I both graduated in the summer of 2002. She graduated from Hughes High School with
a 3.74 G.P.A. and is now attending Ohio State University. I
graduated from Antonelli College with a 4.0 G.P.A. I thank

God for the opportunity to receive a college degree, for going with me everyday, and showing me that with God (and only with God) *all things are possible.* I thank him for all the prayer sessions I shared with my favorite instructor, the Director of Business Office Technology, Pam Bingham. That's right we had many prayer and praise breaks at the college.

Hopefully my testimony will encourage you to go and accomplish that which you once thought was unobtainable or impossible. Jesus paid an awesome price to allow you the opportunity to live life to the fullest. I'm not speaking about having an abundance of things. I'm talking about righteousness, peace and joy (Kingdom living) in the Holy Ghost.

No I haven't moved into a great new job making lots of money. There are still people who won't acknowledge, hire, or receive me even with a College Degree. God allowed me to go to school to raise my self-confidence. But guess what, once you know Jesus, King of Kings and Lord of Lords, it's no longer about your self-confidence. Your confidence is in him and him alone and rightfully so!!!

Father God,

My prayer for this reader is that they'd be encouraged to go after that dream you placed in them. Lord, help them to realize that you've placed everything they'll need to accomplish it within them.

In Jesus Name,
Amen

Chapter 14

Single Parents

The bible details many barren Old Testament women. Barrenness is the inability to give birth. Genesis 11: *But Sarai was barren, she had no child.* Genesis 25: *And Isaac intreated the Lord for his wife, because she was barren; and the Lord was intreated of him and Rebekah his wife conceived.* Judges 13: *And there was a certain man of Zorah, of the family of the Danites, whose name was Manoah; and his wife was barren, and bare not. And the angel of the Lord appeared unto the woman, and said unto her, Behold now, thou art barren; and bearest not; but thou shalt conceive and bear a son.* I Samuel 1: *But unto Hannah he gave a worthy portion; for he loved Hannah, but the Lord had shut up her womb. And her adversary provoked her sore, for to make her fret, because the Lord had shut up her womb.* Barrenness was considered a type of curse. Thereby producing a lot of heartache. These women were married with loving husbands, yet that didn't diminish their longing desire to give birth to a child.

Today's woman has an advantage and is able to use new technological methods to conceive. Yet there are still many women who are childless and many fertility doctors working diligently to that end. God instituted family in Genesis 1: *And God blessed them, and God said unto them, Be fruitful, and multiply and replenish the earth.* God wanted married parents raising their children. He wanted those children to grow up in a loving environment. The benefits produced in that environment would ripple through the family and ultimately into society. If you grew up in that type of family environment you're blessed.

Today's issue is Single Parenting. There are many reasons for being a single parent. In some cases it was a mutual decision, in others it was the result of death or divorce, in some unique instances it was rape. And yes there are some who were never asked to marry. You're the only one that knows why you're a single parent. The reason is irrelevant. The relevant issue is that there's a child that needs your affection, discipline, guidance, love, nurturing, patience, understanding, and a lot of your money. Single parenting is a type of barrenness because, in most cases, the desire for the loving assistance of the other parent is overwhelming. It's unfortunate when a parent feels that, since that couples relationship is over, there should be no communication with the child of that relationship.

Although there are male single parents, the majority of single parents are women. Single parenting challenges include being totally responsible for meeting what Maslow terms a hierarchy of needs. His method classifies human needs and motivations into five categories in ascending order of importance: physiological, safety, social, esteem and self-actualization. A single parent often feels depressed, lonely, and overwhelmed. Many times it seems unbearable and if I'm to be painfully honest, sometimes not worth all the sacrifice.

I read a scripture in Matthew 6: *The light of the body is the eye: if therefore thine eye be single, thy whole body shall be full of light.* Children seem to know how to manipulate conversations and sometimes even circumstances to get what they want. In other words, if Daddy says no, then I'll ask Mommy and vice-versa. That speaks to the significance of the eye being single. The eye represents a view. When both parents, living together or apart, can operate with the same single view, it's beneficial to the entire family. In other words, these parents are consistent in their stance of raising their child.

I thought of couples with shared parenting. It's amazing how an established foundation is so easily destroyed in just one weekend visit. It's unfortunate when that absentee parent allows their child to participate in liberties that aren't allowed in the custodial parents home. After that visit the custodial parent now has to, like Nehemiah, rebuild the wall. If you share parenting make sure that you're both on one accord even if you're not in one place.

Oftentimes I think of Mary's immaculate conception. I'm sure that during her pregnancy she faced many of the same concerns that single parents face. Although Joseph was told about her child, Jesus, he wasn't the biological father. Her case was even more unique in that she was engaged when she was found to be with child. Her question

in Luke 1: *How shall this be seeing that I know not a man?*
What a profound statement. This knowing is an intimate
knowing. There are so many women who feel that they are
incomplete unless they are in a relationship, knowing a
man. They ask how can I feel happy, content, and satisfied
with my life seeing that I know not a man? Society says
that at this age I should be happily married, with two children and a beautiful house with a white picket fence. I'm
not even dating. However it's good to know not a man until you have known the best man, Jesus. A relationship with
Jesus will teach you how to love and more importantly who
to love. Today, due to sexual promiscuity, the question,
asked by some woman, is "Whose can this be, seeing that I
know many men?" If Bruce, George, Paul, Bryan, and Bobby
had known Mary, guess who wouldn't have been Jesus'
mother? God needed a pure womb. Luke 1: *And the angel
came in unto her, and said, Hail, thou art highly favoured, the
Lord is with thee; blessed art thou among women."* It goes on
to say: *and the angel said unto her, Fear not, Mary for thou
has found favor with God.* God is still looking for pure vessels to birth his manifestations through.

Yes, Mary was blessed and highly favoured yet she still
had to be delivered. Luke 2: *And so it was, that, while they
were there, the days were accomplished that she should be delivered.* She was exceptionally blessed because she had the
extraordinary advantage of delivering her deliverer. She also
had to receive the Holy Ghost after being delivered. Acts 1:
*And when they were come in, they went up into an upper room,
where abode Peter, and James, and John, and Andrew, Philip,
and Thomas, Bartholomew, and Matthew, James the son of
Alphaeus, and Simon Zelotes, and Judas, the brother of James.*

These all continued with one accord in prayer and supplication with the women, and Mary the mother of Jesus, and with his brethren. Although it's good to blessed and highly favoured the expedient thing is to saved.

I've been a single parent for a lot of years. My mother-in law, Evelyn Welcome King, was born on June 13 and passed in August 1985. My mother, Grace Victoria Charles, was born on June 15 and passed in January 1986. Their deaths, within five months of each other, made an already unbearable situation, even more so. However I wouldn't have been able to leave New York if either of them were alive. They wouldn't have wanted us to be in another state. At that point, my father Alvin Charles and father-in-law Henry King Jr. were more concerned with my mental stability; and the children being raised in a nurturing environment.

I'm a single parent because I chose to take control of a life that I'd relinquished control of. I thank God that, my cousin, Doreen Smith, lovingly convinced me to move from New York to Cincinnati on December 7, 1986. If my children were only going to have one parent, then I needed to be the best single parent I could be. Oswald Chambers wrote in his classic devotional, "My Utmost for His Highest," "The test of a saint is not success, but faithfulness in human life, as it actually is. A key for success is your ability to deal with human life as it is. We put forth so much effort trying to create the life we want. That's fine but not if we aren't dealing with where we presently are. Children become a product of their environment. Therefore, the best place for me (and my children) to be the best we could be was Cincinnati.

Children are important to and a gift from God. We must take responsibility for our children. One of the best things we can do is bring our children to (the knowledge of) Jesus. Matthew 19: *Then there were brought unto him little children, that he should put his hands on them, and pray: and the disciples rebuked them. But Jesus said, Suffer little children, and forbid them not, to come unto me, for of such is the kingdom of heaven.* When parents let Jesus put his hands on their children and pray they won't have to worry about anyone else putting their hands on those children. Jesus promises in Matthew 18: *But whoso shall offend one of these little ones which believe in me, it were better for him that a millstone were hanged about his neck, and that he were drowned in the depth of the sea.* Matthew 20: *Then came to him (Jesus) the mother of Zebedee's children and her sons, worshipping him and desiring a certain thing of him.* Motives are very important to God. I do understand that why you do what you do is more important than what you do. However, we must give her credit because she brought her children to Jesus. Have you? It's commendable that she didn't send them; she brought them. A lot of parents bring or send their children to church and that's good. However this mother brought her children to Jesus, not to church. Jesus should always be their final destination. Guess what, after you get them to him, he's able to take them the rest of the way.

Statistics say that children of single parents grow up with all types of unresolved issues and are rarely successful in their adult lives. Love is all they really need. It's good to have two parents and a nice house etc., but love makes up the shortage when those conditions aren't present. Since most single parents don't receive child support, they often work two, sometimes three jobs in order to meet their financial obligations. Therefore their children spend a lot of time alone or with the overworked babysitter, the television.

Conversely today's woman has made strides in social, political and economic arenas. Many women enjoy the success of a high-powered job. These women are able to meet and exceed their financial obligations without financial assistance from the absentee parent. However there can be a high cost for success. These women also spend a lot of time away from their children. Others work from home, but they're busy on the phone, their laptop, or keeping up with appointments using their palm pilot. Don't let your career commitments take quality time away from your child. Their young years are their formative years. Once that child's foundation has been laid, you'll have the satisfaction of knowing that, your child will always obey, not as in your presence only, but now much more in your absence. Now is a specific time and means that something preceded it and that something made the now possible.

Some successful career-focused parents bestow materialism instead of time on their children. The bible says in Proverbs 22: *Train up a child in the way he should go and when he is old he shall not depart from it.* In order to train, the trainee must spend quality time with the trainer. The bible says train up a child. This denotes growth and helping that child advance from immaturity to maturity. The bible doesn't say give the child a train. Today's children have so much, however the bible says in Luke 12: *for a man's life consisteth not in the abundance of the things which he possesseth.*

Single Parents, let me encourage you. God loves your child more than you do. He knew, that with his help, you would raise a child that you both would be very proud of.

I'll lend you for a little while, A child of mine, God said. But there are lessons taught below, I want this child to learn I've looked the whole world over, in my search for teachers true And from the things that crowd life's lane, I HAVE CHOSEN YOU!!!!!!!
Now will you give her/him all your love?

Guess what, after it's all said and done the only thing that will matter to God and your child is the answer to this question "Did your child feel loved, or left?"

Father God,

My prayer for this reader is that you'd make them very aware that there's no challenge to difficult for you. Lord, help them to learn how to lean on you.

In Jesus Name,
Amen

Chapter 15

The Ring

The date was October 12, 2000. That morning I'd driven to Norwood, parked in the Surrey Square Mall, and taken the bus to school. That afternoon I got off the bus put my book bag in my car and went into Thriftway. There was a gentleman being waited on by one of the cashiers. As I briskly walked by he said "Hello gorgeous." I smiled, replied "Hi" and kept walking. I remembered a time in my life when that greeting would've made my day. Those days, I wouldn't go to the mailbox or even take the garbage out without being in my opinion "gorgeous." However even then I realized that looking gorgeous didn't make me feel that way. God had since done a work in me and his presence in my life made me feel gorgeous.

In 1997 I was employed at Gibson Greetings Inc. and would have lunch in my car. There, I'd listen to sermon tapes and/or gospel music, and pray without being disturbed. During one of those lunch periods I'd told the Lord that I'd give up anything for him. I can still hear his voice, saying, "Take the lipstick off." My spirit had just surrendered all and yet I now quickly realized that my flesh had only surrendered some. The spirit was willing but the flesh was weak. As a matter of fact, flesh wanted to wait until the end of the week to surrender because it could stay in all weekend. The Lord was teaching me that I was in bondage to anything I couldn't give up or take off. I replied OK Lord and wiped the lipstick off. I returned from lunch feeling quite ugly. It seemed as though everyone was looking at me and that I looked pretty bad. I recently read in Jeremiah 1: *be not dismayed at their faces.* They were obviously dismayed at my face and I was equally dismayed by the look on theirs. Looks, like words, can kill and/or make you want to kill. I wish I had been acquainted with that scripture back then.

However by that October day I'd been made free from my desperate need to be attractive to man. I'd realized that real freedom isn't the ability to do whatever you want to do; real freedom is your ability to choose not to. I was actually dressing down, no lipstick, and no earrings. I knew Jesus loved me just the way I was and that I was complete in him. Now back to the story. I was shopping in one of the aisles and he approached me. He asked my name. I replied "Victoria." He informed me that his name was Edward. He asked if we could exchange telephone numbers. I replied that I'd be willing to take his number. I chose not to give mine. He gave his home and work number(s). Since he gave both numbers I figured that he wasn't married and didn't have a live-in girlfriend. He was also employed. That's always good. He left and I kept shopping. I had no intention of calling him.

The Lord kept bringing him to my remembrance. One morning in prayer, I asked "Lord, what is it about him?" "You know I just started school." "I don't have time to date or start a relationship." Why do we feel the need to inform or update God? He's never once said, "Thanks Victoria, I didn't know that." After a period of travailing my spirit finally realized that it wasn't even about me. I repented and told God that I was sorry. "God, if this is about you then I'll call." I came out of my prayer closet and picked up one of my daily devotionals. I'm usually a few days behind in the reading. I started reading at the beginning of that week. The devotional for October 12 amazed me because it read, "The next person you meet may need to meet Jesus." Wow! I vowed to call him.

I wasn't sure if he had Caller ID so I called from work on a Saturday. I placed the call with the intention of being off the phone within two minutes. We are so funny. I had told the Lord I would call. I didn't tell him I'd engage in a lengthy conversation. I would've ended that brief conversation feeling very proud because I'd done what I vowed. I informed Edward that I was at work and began my attempt to end the conversation. He chimed in with a question. "When can we get together?" I replied, "I'm busy, very busy, very, very busy." God must have given him this response. He replied, "Are you to busy to eat?" Now you can look at (all of) me and see I'm not too busy to eat. I sheepishly replied, "I try to eat everyday." I was going to school full-time and only working twenty-one hours a week. Lord knows my response was the truth! He then asked if we could go out to dinner. I agreed. We arranged to meet after work on Friday. I told the Lord that we were going out. Another update. The devotional reading stated that Edward needed to meet Jesus. Therefore I decided that I'd spend the entire evening talking about Jesus. I always carry my bible, but I also took a few written scriptures to use for conversational purposes. I knew that would be my (first and) last supper with Edward.

During our conversation, at Cookers in Tri-County, I tried to find out where he was spiritually. He seemed to have some knowledge of the word. That surprised me. During dinner I mentioned how corny that gorgeous line was. He stated that I did look gorgeous. He went on to say that "I looked clean" and that "there appeared to be a light around me." I thought, "He has gone where no man should go." My next thought was "Lord get me home quick." Actually we finished dinner and then rode across the river to Kentucky for the super sale. We had spent all evening talking about Jesus and I had enjoyed myself. After we left the super sale, he drove me to Kenwood to get my car and we parted.

The next morning in prayer, I asked, "Lord, I thought he needed to meet you? "He seemed to know a lot about you." It was during that prayer time that I understood my looking clean and the light he mentioned. October 12 was my spiritual birthday. Three years earlier I had received the gift of the Holy Ghost. God allowed him to see the light that comes from his children. I had to repent, again, for believing Edward was just coming up with some line. We talked more frequently. During one of our conversations, he asked if there was a man in my life. I told him emphatically YES!!!! I went on to say that "his name is Jesus and you can't take his place." I was so bold about Jesus. There was something on the inside working on the outside. He just laughed. I wasn't the first female who talked about Jesus so he figured it would come to pass. I thought, "You'll come to pass before my Jesus will."

Each time he called I talked about Jesus. I love Jesus like that! During one of our conversations, I mentioned that I'd read Matthew 8: *The centurion answered and said Lord, I am not worthy that thou shouldest come under my roof, but speak the word only and my servant shall be healed.* I went on to say that scripture really blessed me. I realized that most people don't want your opinion, even when they ask for it. They just want you to agree with them. Now I would "speak the word only", in other words respond with biblical answers. After all everything is in the book. Sister Wade says it best. "It's like Prego, it's in there." I guess that was the straw that broke the camels back. That really bothered him. He called me an EXTREMIST and stated that everyone doesn't want to hear the word all the time. I replied that I'd been an extremist in the world. I'd finally met Jesus. How much more should I be now? Jesus deserves me to be an extremist for him. His comment didn't bother me. I was actually glad. Matthew 5: *Blessed are ye, when men shall revile you, and persecute you, and shall say all manner of evil against you falsely, for my sake.*

During our conversations I was crystal clear about my celibacy. I was waiting to share that intimacy with my next husband. He replied "you'll be single the rest of your life; because no one buys a dress without trying it on first." I responded, "no one asked you to buy this dress." The interesting thing was that I didn't think I would ever marry again. Yes, that means that I was willing to live the rest of my life celibate. I'd already told him about being baptized in Jesus name and the infilling of the Holy Ghost with the evidence of speaking in tongues. Although he wasn't going for any of that, I knew that Jesus is a keeper. Oh yes he is!

Each time he called I was surprised. He often commented on my dress and my fanaticism regarding my relationship with Jesus. Initially he made many hurtful comments. However, God had already equipped me. He couldn't shake my faith. Jack, or in my case, Jackie was already out of the box. God started drawing him. I mentioned earlier that the devotional reading stated that the next person you meet may need to meet Jesus. He knew of God, but he didn't know God. He began to study the Sunday school lessons with me. He admitted that he first started reading the bible to "bring something to the table." He probably wanted to shut me up. God's word is true therefore Edward's desire for it and God's presence developed quickly. God allowed me to see him change.

In April 2001, he picked me up from school and asked if we could go to the park for a little while. He seemed to have something on his mind. We found a quiet place and parked. He said, "I want to ask you something" and began to reach for this little gold metallic bag. He began to pull a ring box out of it. I never allowed him to take the box out its little bag. I said that I wasn't ready for him to ask me THAT question. I suggested he keep his ring. I apologized and informed him that I wasn't rejecting him. I explained that I was committed to God and my promise to complete college. I was unable to commit to anything else.

He accepted my reply and took me home. We parted and to be honest, I thought I'd never hear from him again. Later on that evening he called. He stated that he'd purchased that ring for me and that he wanted me to have it. He said I could wear it as a friendship ring. I was very honest. I told him that since he wanted me to have it, I'd take it. Nevertheless, I informed him that I wouldn't wear it until I was ready to wear it for the purpose with which he'd given it. When I finally saw the ring I almost fell off my seat. It is beautiful. All I could think of was look at God. It pays to serve him. All I had given up was good conversation and I was rewarded with this beautiful diamond ring. Philippians 1: *Only let your conversation be as it becometh the gospel of Christ: that whether I come and see you, or else be absent, I may hear of your affairs, that ye stand fast in one spirit, with one mind striving together for the faith of the gospel.*

It's interesting because at first Edward didn't think my conversation was that good. I wasn't saying anything that he wanted to hear. This was truly a situation for revelation. I teach a bible study class at work and because of that situation God gave me a lesson entitled "Don't let a GOOD thing, keep you from a GOD thing!" A God thing is your assignment from God. Many times, while standing for that God thing, you're presented with a good thing. That good thing may (and is often designed by Satan to) lead you astray. I told my class that emotion causes many to give up the God thing for what appears to be a good thing. Your biological clock is ticking (fast); you feel it's not just a good thing; it's a very good thing. It's never good to give up a God thing. Here are a few thoughts included in that lesson:

- God gave commandments, not suggestions!
- Most of the time, things that look good to us aren't good for us!
- Every Good idea is not a God idea!
- It doesn't take very long to realize that your Good idea wasn't a God idea!
- Everything good isn't God, but God is everything good!

I went on to mention that God didn't want me to look at the ring. My wedding ring was pretty but it was about a half size too small. When it was time to exchange rings my sister stood behind me with a small jar of Vaseline. I placed my finger in the Vaseline before Kevin placed the ring on my finger. That should have been a clue huh? God knew that if I'd seen Edward's ring, I would have remembered the challenge presented by Kevin's ring. I probably would've said yes just because of that. Please understand! I'm not against marriage. I grew up watching Cinderella, she married the Prince and they lived happily ever after. I married a "King" and had even greater expectations. I'm saying that marriage outside of God's timing and will isn't a God thing.

I hope my story encourages women and men to stand for God and know that he's able to do as stated in Ephesians 3: *Now unto him that is able to do exceeding abundantly above all that we ask or think, according to the power that worketh in us.*

God has blessed Edward. Elder Lavelton Daniel baptized him in Jesus name on September 5, 2001. He has such a wonderful testimony about his baptism. He said that afterwards he felt so light, almost as if he was floating. He didn't feel his foot touching the pedals as he drove home. I reminded him that the baptism in Jesus name was for the remission of sin. The name of Jesus is a cleansing name. He felt light because his sins were now remissed. The devil has a way of disguising the weight of sin. Prior to his baptism Edward wasn't aware of how heavy his sin was. That feeling of weightlessness after his baptism made the knowledge of that weight very apparent. Shortly thereafter he was filled with the Holy Ghost evidenced by his speaking in other tongues. He now speaks more word than me. God has made him an EXTREMIST! Glory to God! He will fight and win your battle!

God had told me from the beginning that Edward needed to meet him and I was accountable for that. I thank God for the opportunity to help someone meet him. Proverbs 11: *The fruit of the righteous is a tree of life; and he that winneth souls is wise.* The best way to win souls is with your lifestyle: living what the word says. Yes, Edward and I are still friends. God has blessed us with a spiritual love that is far better than any other.

I never knew life could be so, so complete
With just one look in your eyes,
no one else has ever made me feel unique with no
strings or compromise
We're inseparable only to find that we're growing
closer through time.
Cause we have a spiritual love that lasts for a
lifetime
Spiritual Love
Trin-I-Tee 5:7

I recently traveled to New York and was engaged in a conversation with my relatives. I took my ring to show them. They were trying to understand my relationship with Edward and my inability to commit to marriage. They commented that I obviously didn't love him. That's not it. I just love God more and have to fulfill the spiritual destiny that he's purposed for my life. When I began to realize that they weren't able to understand my feelings, I said "Goodnight" and proceeded to go upstairs to bed. As I walked up the steps, the Holy Ghost said in my spirit "You're the one with the ring!!!!!" In other words, it doesn't matter whether they understand or not. What does matter is your obedience to me and that Edward understands your feelings and still wants you to have his ring. Every once in a while, I take my ring out to look at it. When I do, I'm reminded of how great God is and how blessed I am to be loved by him and Edward.

Father God,

My prayer for this reader is that you'd help them identify their God thing and that they'd, forsaking any good thing, be willing to accomplish it. Lord, help them to see that you have something even better than a ring for them; you have a crown of righteousness.

In Jesus Name,
Amen

Chapter 16

Prepare for Take-off

We recently traveled to New York. I thank God that, even after September 11, I never feared getting on the plane. I'd been so busy preparing for the trip that I hadn't realized that I'd be going into downtown New York City. I wasn't sure how I'd handle being where the tragedy occurred. I felt sad because of the many lost lives, broken hearts, and unanswered questions. However I was excited about the trip and seeing my family. I mentally prepared myself for the lengthy airport process due to the stricter security measures. The day finally arrived. Our flight from Columbus to New York was canceled twice. We were examined and practically x-rayed even before our new flight was determined. We finally got on a plane. Initially we had a straight flight but after the cancellations, we had a layover in Boston. Anytime you venture off Straight Street there is the possibility of a layover.

My stomach began to feel queasy as we ascended. Then I heard it. The Holy Ghost said "the higher you go the easier it gets." That was very comforting and spiritually sound. I realized that initially our relationship with God is uncomfortable. The Christian walk is a high way because we serve the most High God. *Deuteronomy 2: Let me pass through thy land: I will go along by the high way; I will neither turn unto the right hand nor to the left. Psalm 71: Thy righteousness also O God, is very high, who hast done great things: O God, who is like unto thee! Psalm 138: Though the Lord be high, yet hath he respect unto the lowly,* (Thank God) *but the proud he knoweth afar off. Psalm 149: Let the high praises of God be in their mouth, and a twoedged sword in their hand.* The Holy Ghost was right because the higher we go, the more we see God! Seeing God makes everything easier.

Soon we were above the clouds. Things that once appeared very large were now very small. I thought God is a wonder. Those clouds looked like big cotton balls. It was absolutely beautiful. *Romans 1: For the invisible things of him from the creation of the world are clearly seen, being understood by the things that are made, even his eternal power and Godhead, so that they are without excuse.* I spent the rest of the time staring out the window trying to comprehend the awesomeness of God. The comforting words from the Holy Ghost and the view made all the hassles worth it.

In Matthew 6 Jesus made five references to the same phrase. That phrase is "Take No Thought." It's referenced as, taking thought, take ye thought, take no thought saying and finally take therefore no thought. Those verses should typify our relationship with God. They speak to our concern for our life, what we shall eat, what we shall drink, and what we shall put on. We've spent and do spend a lot of time thinking about those very things. The more time we spend with him the smaller worldly concerns become. It's our fear of not having those things that concern us. 1 John 4: *There is no fear in love and that perfect love casteth out fear, because fear hath torment. He that feareth is not made perfect in love.* Therefore whenever I began to feel fear then I have to analyze the love that I say I have for God. If I really love him, then I must trust him and that trust has to dispel fear.

We're all familiar with II Timothy 1: *For God hath not given us the spirit of fear; but of power, and of love, and of a sound mind.* That's right fear is a spirit, which doesn't come from God. However fear and faith have a common component. They both challenge you to believe in something unseen. The world says fear is F-alse E-vidence A-ppearing R-eal. God gave me a spiritual acronym for fear. It is F-orever E-mbrace the A-uthority of R-edeemer. At first I didn't understand that. Who embraces authority? What he shared was that when fear comes, I have to embrace or understand that no one or no thing can deter my redeemer's ability.

God blessed me with another spiritual revelation coming back. We were now traveling from New York to Columbus. Surprisingly the security procedures at the New York Airport were less strenuous. We checked our luggage, went through the exams and boarded the train. Although the process was less strenuous it was still very thorough. It was bearable because we'd gone through it so many times on the flights traveling to New York. Practice makes (us) perfect or better able to deal with discomforts.

The Lord showed me how easily we put our trust in man when we've paid for our right to something. I realized that the passenger's confidence is in the fact that they'd secured their right to travel from one destination to another. Therefore that airline is obligated to get them to their destination, one-way or the other. The Reverend Dr. Susan Newman records, in her book OH GOD! "We will get on an airplane that some unknown people made and let a strange crew take us thirty thousand feet into the sky. We trust that the stranger in the cockpit knows what he's doing." That flight taught me that the carrier is obligated to get us to our destination but there are no guarantees. The realization made me appreciate my relationship with a God who holds all guarantees.

The male flight attendant made a three-minute speech. It was obvious that he'd made it many times before. After he did so, I heard something that really blessed me. The pilot requested that we prepare for take-off. That hit my spirit hard. We felt that once we received our tickets we were prepared. The Holy Ghost began to show me that, even after purchasing the tickets, being checked out in order to check in, to walk on, and then be strapped in, we were still not prepared for take-off. That's the problem with religious people. They go through processes but they never prepare for take-off. They're satisfied with staying on the ground. God wants his people prepared for take-off in order to run with patience the race that is set before them.

I Chronicle 29: *O LORD God of Abraham, Isaac, and of Israel, our fathers, keep this for ever in the imagination of the thoughts of the heart of thy people, and prepare their heart unto thee*: Isaiah 40: *The voice of him that crieth in the wilderness, Prepare ye the way of the LORD, make straight in the desert a highway for our God.* Ezekiel 38: *Be thou prepared, and prepare for thyself, thou, and all thy company that are assembled unto thee, and be thou a guard unto them.* Amos 4: *Therefore thus will I do unto thee, O Israel: and because I will do this unto thee, prepare to meet thy God, O Israel.*

The interesting thing is that even after the passengers had prepared for take-off; the plane was still unable to take off. The plane just taxied on the runaway. After a period of time the air traffic controller said, "You can now take off." Now always indicates a specific time! Not then but now. That's a truth that we all need to learn if we want to do anything for the Lord. Once you've prepared be willing to wait for your "Now" word from God. We are unable to accomplish expedient results when the right thing is done at the wrong time.

How do you prepare? You have to develop an ear to hear God's voice when he speaks to you. The bible records seven references in Revelation 2 & 3: *He that hath an ear let him hear what the Spirit saith unto the churches.* We are the church. Many times we're more concerned about hearing a specific speaker than with hearing the Spirit spoken through ANY speaker. Let's look at a biblical illustration of someone who was willing to wait. In Genesis 24: *And the man wondering at her held his peace, to wit whether the Lord had made his journey prosperous or not.* (His task was to find a wife for Isaac. His prayer requested the satisfying of specific criteria. The bible says *before he had done speaking (to God) that behold Rebekah came out.* Even though Rebekah spoke those things he'd prayed for, he still held his peace). Glory! He knew it was God but he just wanted to be sure. He was willing to wait to make sure his blessing was indeed coming from God and that it was the answer to his prayer! Are you? Ecclesiastes 3: *To every thing there is a season, and a time to every purpose under the heaven.*

Again, even after we've done all we can and feel sure about God's provision we must still wait and get permission from God before actually taking off. Otherwise you've went without being sent. The question is how do we prepare? Our church, Greater Emanuel Apostolic Temple, was recently expanded and renovated. I must admit it's beautiful. We had a meeting to prepare for our Grand Opening. A lot of information was shared and a concern was voiced about all the efforts being put forth to make that opening successful. Evangelist Trish Daniel stood up to respond and said something that's still blessing me. She said, "We are trying to do things a cut above the rest." Glory to God! We serve an awesome God who is a cut above the rest and he desires to make us a cut above the rest. Therefore when we are representing him we must do things a cut above the rest. (Thank you Trish, that has really blessed me. Here I was feeling bad cause I've never heard you preach. If that's any indication, preach girl, preach!). Be willing to elevate your mindset. Oswald Chambers, author of My Utmost For His Highest, put it this way "The viewpoint of a worker for God must not be as near the highest as he can get, it must be the highest."

We do that by having an open, willing, and obedient heart to receive ALL the things of God from ALL the word of God. Then we prepare by spending time with God and in his word. Our old thoughts, perceptions, traditions, and mindsets must be done away with. This is a process and isn't accomplished overnight. Be patient! Realize that it can be done when and if we allow God's word and his voice to be the final authority.

Father God,

My prayer for this reader is that you'd prepare them to be willing to take-off into the spiritual destiny you've designed especially for them.

In Jesus Name,
Amen

Chapter 17

The Lifeguard

P rayer is a tool that provides access to God. Most of the chapters in my book were derived from time spent in prayer. I moved here from New York. Although I have lived in Cincinnati for sixteen years, I still have my New York accent. I am often asked, "Where are you from?" My response is "I'm from my mother." I've grown accustomed to the looks I receive after that response. The next most frequent question asked of me is "What brought you here? It is so unusual for Cincinnatians to hear that I left the big city of New York to move here. Most people think it's far better to move from Cincinnati to New York. I thank God for this move. My response to that second question is "A plane." I am fully aware of what is meant when asked those questions. However, I humorously answer the questions that were asked. In order to receive the desired response we must ask the right questions.

If this is the case in the natural, it is even more so in the spiritual. Communication with man and more importantly with God is the best way to learn how to ask correct questions. What do I mean? Well people that know my warped sense of humor know how to question me. In speaking certain words, like coffee, talk, and aunt, my accent is very distinctive. One morning in prayer I said, "you're my life God." It sounded as if I said you're my lifeguard. I immediately thought about the duties of a lifeguard. They sit high so that they are able to see everything. Therefore at the first indication of trouble they jump down and run (into the water) to offer assistance. Sounds like Jesus, he sits high and looks low! What a spiritual parallel.

At first I laughed, but it didn't take long for me to realize that he is my lifeguard. He guards my life. He said in Isaiah 43: *When you pass through the waters, I will be with you; And through the rivers, they shall not overflow you. When you walk through the fire, you shall not be burned, Nor shall the flame scorch you.* The word of God is right and there is always confirmation of a promise elsewhere in the bible. This scripture is proven in Daniel 3: *And the princes, governors, and captains, and the king's counselors, being gathered together, saw these men, upon whose bodies the fire had no power, nor was an hair of their head singed, neither were their coats changed, nor the smell of fire passed on them.*

I thank him for his declaration in John 10: *The thief does not come but for to steal, and to kill, and to destroy. I have come that they might have life, and that they might have it more abundantly.* When he died on that cross, he was guarding my life. John 3: *God so loved the world that he gave his only begotten Son, so that whosoever believeth in him shall not perish but have everlasting life.* He guarded so many of the Old Testament prophets and even his New Testament disciples. He is even guarding you. I know you thought it was luck that kept that car, those drugs, or those friendly enemies from killing you. Oh no, it was God. Jeremiah 29: *For I know the thoughts that I think toward you, says the Lord, thoughts of peace and not of evil, to give you a future and a hope.* Although this statement was directed to Jeremiah, I believe that scripture to be true in the lives of all God's children.

I am so glad that God is the giver of all life. John 1: *All things were made by him; and without him was not any thing made that was made. In him was life and the life was the light of men.* John 6: *Verily, verily I say unto you He that believeth on me hath everlasting life. I am the bread of life.*

In conclusion, God is indeed my lifeguard and for that I give him all the praise! I am so grateful that as long as I love him with all my mind, heart, and soul that I am able to claim this promise:

Romans 8: *Who shall separate us from the love of Christ? Shall tribulation, or distress, or persecution, or famine, or nakedness, or peril, or sword? As it is written, FOR THY SAKE WE ARE KILLED ALL THE DAY LONG; WE ARE AC-COUNTED AS SHEEP FOR THE SLAUGHTER. Nay, in all these things we are more than conquerors through him that loved us. For I am persuaded, that neither death, nor life, nor angels, nor principalities, nor powers, nor things present, nor things to come. Nor height, nor depth, nor any other creature, shall be able to separate us from the love of God, which is in Christ Jesus our Lord.*

Father God,

My prayer for this reader is that they'd recognize the many times you've guarded their life from dangers seen and unseen. Lord, help them to turn that life over to you.

In Jesus Name,
Amen

Chapter 18

Jesus Paid to Know You!

There are many ways to pay for something. You can pay with your time, with labor, with cash, and some pay with their body, which produces heartache, heartbreak, grief, loneliness, and tears. When I was in school, female students would say that they'd only go out with someone who was good-looking, had a nice car, and a good job. I thought some of these students would never get a date. I felt that those things shouldn't be a prerequisite if you care for a person. I always wanted a person to care for me and want to be in my presence because of me and not because of the things I possessed.

A lot of those girls would get dates with those types of guys. They'd come back and brag about the places they'd gone to, the money given to them, and the money spent on their behalf. In some cases, a few months later I'd find that they'd also been given another present, which now resulted in the form of a round presence. It was different in bible days. I am reminded of the stories in Genesis 2: God brought Eve to Adam, and in Genesis 24 *when Abraham instructed his eldest servant "to swear by the Lord, that thou shalt not take a wife unto my son of the daughters of the Canaanites."* In Genesis 29: *Jacob served Laban for seven years for Rachel his younger daughter.*

The attitude of those female students is still around today. Some are still selecting men based on their own fleshly desires and needs, for perceived prestige, or as I term it "Social Security benefits." However, in some cases, financial gain isn't an issue. A large number of today's women are making more money than some men. There was a commercial whose slogan was "You've come a long way baby." Amen. I recently watched an episode of Law and Order. Henry Winkler, (better known as Fonzi or The Fonz) married a wealthy older woman. He then had her raped and almost killed in order to inherit her money. Initially, regardless of all the evidence, she didn't believe he was involved. She said, "He made me feel special." While doing so he was also looking around at all the special things she had. He'd selected her because of her wealth. Statistics had determined that there were at least seven to ten women to each man. Some men are making sure they're involved with every one of them. A very popular song was entitled "What's Love Got to Do With It? That's today's mentality. Other women, regardless of their financial status, still manage to take care of the men they love or hope to marry.

As a single woman I'm very aware of how society makes single women feel. God wants everyone to recognize that even if there is no Joe, Bob, Glenn, Bruce, Walter or Sean in your life, YOU ARE STILL VALUABLE AND LOVED. God is the greatest lover in the world and he proved that by providing himself as a sacrificial lamb in the form of Jesus. Colossians 2: *For in him (Jesus) dwelleth all the fulness of the Godhead bodily.* Hebrews 10: *But this man, after he had offered one sacrifice for sins for ever, sat down on the right hand of God.* Jesus was the only one who could do that for us.

John 13: *Now before the feast of the Passover, when Jesus knew that his hour was come and that he should depart out of this world unto the Father, having loved his own which were in the world, he loved them unto the end.* Take a few moments and think about when or if you were ever loved unto the end. I don't mean the end of the hour, day, month, or the year. Some relationships are just that short and if I'm to be really honest, it was never about love. It was about another four-letter word beginning with the letter "L" and that word is lust. I meant until the end of that person's life.

Let me go back to the story of Rachel. Love pays for you by working for you while waiting seven years to be with you. If you read Genesis 29 you'll find that Jacob was actually deceived and given Leah instead of Rachel. He then had to wait another week for Rachel and then work for another seven years. Now that's love. God loves even better! The bible is a love story. There is another love story about Hosea and Gomer.

Hosea 1: *And the LORD said to Hosea, Go, take unto thee a wife of whoredoms and children of whoredoms: for the land hath committed great whoredom, departing from the LORD.* God loves obedience and the next verse says *"So he went and took Gomer the daughter of Diblaim; which conceived, and bare him a son."* Hosea 3: *Then said the LORD unto me, Go yet, love a woman beloved of her friend, yet an adulteress, according to the love of the LORD toward the children of Israel, who look to other gods, and love flagons of wine." So I bought her to me for fifteen pieces of silver, and for an homer of barley, and an half homer of barley: And I said unto her, Thou shalt abide for me many days; thou shalt not play the harlot, and thou shalt not be for another man: so will I also be for thee.* God was demonstrating the depth of real love and the extent it should be willing to go. A whore or an adulteress is normally not chosen for long-term companionship in a respectable relationship. Look at God, some of us were those things and even worse yet God still loved us enough to redeem us with his own blood!

Luke 15: *And he arose, and came to his father. But when he was yet a great way off, his father saw him, and had compassion, and ran, and fell on his neck, and kissed him. And the son said unto him, Father, I have sinned against heaven, and in thy sight, and am no more worthy to be called thy son. But the father said to his servants, Bring forth the best robe, and put it on him; and put a ring on his hand, and shoes on his feet. And bring hither the fatted calf, and kill it; and let us eat, and be merry: For this my son was dead, and is alive again; he was lost, and is found. And they began to be merry."* These stories illustrate a type of God's love and his willingness in displaying that love. You are never so low that his love can't reach down and lift you to your rightful place in him.

At the beginning of this chapter I mentioned a few of the different ways we pay for what we feel we want and even need. This book is about the love of Jesus. He came and paid, by shedding his blood, to know you. Now some have been made to shed blood by a scorned man or woman. That's not the shedding of blood I'm referring to. There's no other love like the love of Jesus. Some may have paid with their life (savings). Jesus paid with his life. He says referring to his life in John 10: *No man taketh it from me, but I lay it down of myself. I have power to lay it down, and I have power to take it again.* Yes, he paid to know you and for you to be his bride. You may or may not have been a bride, but there's someone waiting for you to walk down the aisle in your beautiful apparel. He says, with tears in his eyes, there she is. There's the one that I died to have. I hope she loves and wants me as much as I love and want her.

Bishop recently lost the lovely woman he'd been married to for 45 years. This past Sunday he made an awesome statement. He said "he's already been a groom so now he's working on being a bride." Glory! That's right, Jesus paid for the entire world. Your sex will not hinder your becoming his bride. I hadn't thought of it that way. You see I have a son named Tony. Thanks to Bishop, I'll tell him that if he keeps working on it, one day he'll also be a bride.

Father God,

My prayer for this reader is that they'd recognize the high price you paid for their presence. Lord, help them to honor you and the things you desire with their life.

In Jesus Name,
Amen

Chapter 19

The Insanity Plea

I have always loved mysteries. When I was younger, I watched all the Perry Mason movies. My children refer to him as Perry. I eventually graduated to Matlock, Murder She Wrote, and Law and Order. Obviously I wasn't the only one, because Law and Order now has three spinoffs. How could I have forgotten another favorite, Columbo! I've often wondered about my fixation with those crime dramas. I now realize that I loved solving the mystery. It's always that one thing the camera focused on or something mentioned in passing. When you recognize the significance of even the smallest detail then that mystery begins to unfold. You're on the way to solving it.

The avenue(s) of defense have always been of interest to me. The defense justifies your actions. That defense is very important because it determines if and how much time you'll have to do if found guilty. If you're caught in the very act, in person, on camera, or with pictures the focus is no longer if you did it, the focus becomes why you did it. In today's society, there are many reasons given. Self-defense is often used. You felt (by threat or implication) that your life was in danger. After all those years of sexual abuse, you had to defend yourself. The word of God is so good. It says that the battle is not yours it's the Lord's. Guess what, he fights much better and always wins.

Another defense that I find interesting is the Insanity Plea. The more heinous the crime, the more this plea is used. After all you had to be insane to walk right up to someone on a crowded street and shoot him or her. You had to be insane to kill your child, or all your children. You had to be insane to try to fly; you had to be insane to attempt to rob that bank with that water gun. To be insane means you've lost control of your mental faculties. We've all done some crazy things. Sometimes we've even felt crazy. Some of your closest associates have even told you that you're insane. That should be a clue, check your company!

I recently watched an episode of Matlock. He was convinced that his client hadn't committed this crime. He also knew who had done so yet he was unable to prove it. The alleged suspect had taken a powerful sedative and because of the dosage she was asleep at the time of the murder. They then discovered that she had a multiple personality. Matlock proved that it's possible for the dominant personality to be awake and alert even when the weaker personality is sedated. It was finally proven that the dominant personality had in fact committed the murder.

Galatians 5: *This I say then, Walk in the Spirit, ye shall not fulfill the lust of the flesh. For the flesh lusteth against the*

Spirit, and the Spirit against the flesh; and these are contrary the one to the other; so that ye cannot do the things ye would. We also have multiple personalities. Our flesh is the dominant personality before we're saved. Afterwards, one personality is led by flesh and the Spirit attempts to lead the other personality. Scripture says that these war one against the other. Sadly, some have been saved for a while and flesh is still the dominant personality. However when we allow our spirit man to become the dominant personality then he is able to perform on our behalf. However he won't be killing people; he'll be killing flesh!

What am I saying? I'm saying that the reason God is willing to save us is because he knows we all have a common defense. That's right "The Insanity Plea." We'd have to be insane to keep living beneath our privileges, to remain in bondage, to be willing to miss out on the Greatest Love and meeting the Greatest Lover. God has given so much on our behalf. Don't allow anyone or anything to keep you from receiving all that he has for you. I believe that "all" to be him. He's enough, because he is the satisfying portion. However in case you are still debating and not sure if you should do the "God thing", then I give you permission to use this "Insanity Plea" defense when you finally come to yourself. I pray that it won't take you too much longer.

I John 2: *My little children, these things I write unto you, that ye sin not. And if any man sin, we have an advocate with the Father, Jesus Christ the righteous.*

Father God,

My prayer for this reader is that they'd need no defense when they come to you. Lord, allow this reader to understand that although you know everything, that everything you know doesn't and shouldn't keep them from coming to you.

In Jesus Name,
Amen

Chapter 20

Work (It) Out

I've always purchased different exercise equipment. My family often teased and laughed at me because they knew that I'd purchased something else that wouldn't work. Purchasing the equipment was the easy part. However since I was impatient, getting dressed, securing the exercise mat, setting up the equipment and beginning the work out was the hard part. It's still amazes me that it took years to acquire these additional inches and pounds, and yet I wanted to exercise a few days and see a noticeable difference in the mirror. I would always start the newest regime with excitement. Most commercials state that results vary depending on the individual. At first I thought that meant that some people didn't have the needed metabolism to obtain their desired result. I loved that thought so much that after about a week of exercising, and no results, I would just attribute it to the fact that I didn't have the right metabolism. Proverbs 21: *Every way of a man is right in his own eyes: but the LORD pondereth the hearts.* I know that's right. I was always able to come up with a thought that would justify my actions.

My children have watched this fitness cycle for years. Once when Tony was home I was working out. That morning he walked by my bedroom, looked in and said, "Ma, you're doing that wrong." (Guess who didn't get breakfast?). I replied NO I am NOT Tony; he replied, "Yes you are Ma." Then he closed my door and went his way. I now realize that he was willing to show me the correct way. However the tone of my response indicated that I wasn't willing to be shown. My nephew Isaiah was visiting and he saw what he thought to be roller blades partially underneath my bed. It was actually my ABSLIDE. He inquired about my roller blades. My sister and daughter both started laughing. I also laughed because it might as well have been roller blades. It surely wasn't producing ABSLIDE results.

My daughter was preparing to leave for her first trimester at Ohio State University in Columbus, OH. We were discussing what I'd be doing with all my spare time. I mentioned that I'd seen a commercial for another exercise program called the Firm. I was going to purchase it because I was sure this one would REALLY work. She looked over at me and said "Mom, why don't you join a gym?" There'll be others there to help you. (She used more tact than Tony and she was given breakfast). I replied that I didn't need to go to a gym. She said "OK Mom" and left. Why am I sharing this with you? No, I don't need any suggestions about an effective exercise regime. I've given up on that. God loves me, all of me, just the way I am. Glory! (I told you I'd come up with something).

Seriously, our muscles are internal. It does take a while for us to see the effects of those rigorous workouts. I became discouraged because I never saw the outward results of what I was sure my actions had worked in. However, I realized that I hadn't been diligent in following the prescribed methods. Therefore I was unable to achieve my goal. I Corinthians 9: *"Know ye not that they which run in a race run all, but one receiveth the prize? So run, that ye may obtain. And every man that striveth for the mastery is temperate in all things. Now they do it to obtain a corruptible crown but we an incorruptible. I therefore so run, not as uncertainly; so fight I, not as one that beateth the air: But I keep under my body, and bring it into subjection; lest that by any means, when I preach to others, I myself should be a castaway.* Run the race to obtain. I now pose a question. What are you trying to obtain? Are you running that race in order to obtain?

Paul says we put much effort into winning man's race just to obtain a corruptible crown, or one that won't last. The bible says in Philippians 2: *Wherefore, my beloved, as ye have always obeyed, not as in my presence only, but now much more in my absence,* **work out** *your own salvation with fear and trembling. For it is God which worketh in you both to will and to do of his good pleasure.* The bible is a book about relationships. They include our relationship to God, our relating to self and our relationship with others. Therefore my challenge to you is to be willing to work out those relational biblical principles in your life.

God came to save us and he purchased that salvation with his own blood. **Seek biblical salvation.** That is God's desired purpose for every life. Jesus said in John 7: "*He that believeth on me as the scriptures hath said, out of his belly shall flow rivers of living waters.*" Are you willing to work out what God has worked in? Many will say they believe. My question is do they believe as the scripture hath said? My Pastor, Bishop Paul A. Bowers, once said, "It's God's heaven, let him tell you how to get there!" We are all familiar with the story about Noah and the Ark. Everyone in the ark was saved. That ark was a type of Jesus Christ.

A well-known pastor preached about Noah. He stated that because Noah kept the information about the impending destruction to himself, he had to build the ark alone. That pastor's point was that when you aren't willing to share information you end up building the ark alone. It's very beneficial to know the word of God for yourself. Genesis 6: God said "*But with thee will I establish my covenant; and thou shalt come into the ark, thou and thy sons, and thy wife and thy sons' wives with thee. Hebrews 11: By faith Noah, being warned of God of things not seen as yet, moved with fear, prepared an ark to the saving of his house; by the which he condemned the world, and became heir of the righteousness which is by faith.* Wow!!!! The bible says in Deuteronomy 4: *Ye shall not add unto the word which I command you, neither shall ye diminish ought from it, that ye may keep the commandments of the Lord your God which I commanded you.*

What am I saying? When God puts a period, we can't change it into a comma and conversely, when he puts a comma, we can't make it a period. II Peter 3: *The Lord is not slack concerning his promise, as some men count slackness; but is longsuffering to us-ward, not willing that any should perish, but that all should come to repentance.* However he realizes, that in Noah's day and in present day, not everyone will be saved. **Don't Miss The Boat DUE TO THE LACK OF ACCURATE BIBLICAL INFORMATION!!!!!!**

Additionally, God has made you for a specific purpose, and he wants you to not only be all that YOU can be, but more importantly to be ALL THAT HE MADE YOU TO BE. This prayer is best summarized using the words of Paul who stated in Ephesians 3: *And to know the love of Christ, which passeth knowledge, that ye might be filled with all the fullness of God.* I adjure you to seek God and all his fullness.

Father God,

My prayer for this reader, as they approach the close of this book, is that it's produced a more fervent desire for them to see your presence in their everyday life. Lord, I pray that they will give you and your biblical principles first place in their life.

In Jesus Name,
Amen

Chapter 21

He Died for Me to Be

I hope you're more aware of the many ways that my Saviour Jesus has blessed you. If you walk away from this reading with nothing else, I pray that I've illustrated my admiration, adoration, gratitude, humbleness, love, respect, and the awe I feel as I realize that the King of Kings and the Lord of Lord's died for me. That's right, it's very personal. He is MY LIFE!!!!! I've often mentioned that very prophetic statement made by Abraham in Gen. 22: *Son, God will provide HIMSELF a lamb.* He demonstrated "The Anticipatory Love of God." As I type the last chapter of this book I have to admit that he's greatly availed and provided himself to me in this endeavor.

Many times we possess a willingness to do yet we don't possess the ability to do and vice-versa. Let me encourage you, the bible says in II Corinthians 8: *For if there be first a willing mind, it is accepted according to that a man hath, and not according to that he hath not.* I'm so grateful that I have a God who has them both and used them to save my soul. Mary had a little lamb; who identified a problem, and then purposed to wrap himself in flesh, go down to earth and become the necessary sacrificial lamb to restore his fallen creature.

Mary was so blessed; she actually kissed the face of God. I wonder if Mary really understood that. Oh how I envy her! I wonder a lot about Jesus. I wonder about his birth, his conception was unique. I believe that his birth was also. Who helped deliver my Saviour? Who was the first one to touch him? Where did they get his clothes? When did he take his first step? How old was he when he first slept all night? What was his first word? I heard someone say that we should be silent where the bible is silent; and speak where the bible speaks. Therefore although I have so many other questions, I'll just wait and ask him when I see him. Glory!

Hebrew 12: *Looking unto Jesus the author and finisher of our faith; who for the joy that was set before him endured the cross, despising the shame, and is set down at the right hand of the throne of God.* Joy, how could the cross be joy? His joy was in knowing that he was saving much people alive. My only regret is my delay in praising him and living a life that he could be proud of. I realize that without his help, I am helpless, hopeless and lifeless. I LOVE HIM! I am willing to die daily that he may get the glory out of a life he changed by his extraordinary love.

One of the greatest controversies in the church is the baptism in Jesus name. I do understand why. I must discuss this in my book. I stated that I wasn't giving verse numbers. However because of the seriousness of this subject I will. The two verses of scripture are respectfully located in Matthew 28:19 and Acts 2:38. The verse in Matthew 28 is in red, which indicates that Jesus spoke it.

Deuteronomy 29:29: The secret things belong unto the LORD our God: but those things which are revealed belong unto us and to our children for ever, that we may do all the words of this law.

Matthew 13:11: *He (Jesus) answered and said unto them, Because it is given unto you to know the mysteries of the kingdom of heaven, but to them it is not given.*

Philippians 2:8–11: *and being found in fashion as a man, he humbled himself, and became obedient unto death, even the death of the cross. Wherefore God also hath highly exalted him, and given him a name which is above every name: that at the name of Jesus every knee should bow, of things in heaven, and things in earth, and things under the earth; and that every tongue should confess that Jesus Christ is Lord, to the glory of God the Father.*

This is how I illustrated it my children. We were at my church, Greater Emanuel Apostolic Temple. I wrote a few of my titles: daughter, sister, wife, mother, aunt, cousin etc. Then I wrote my name underneath. I remember their facial expressions as I handed that paper to them and requested they do the same. After service, they asked Ma, what were you doing? I explained that in our lives we may have many different titles, but we only have one name. They received my explanation without any hesitation or reservation. I'm proud to report that they have both been baptized in Jesus name.

Matthew 28:19: *Go ye therefore, and teach all nations baptizing them in the name of the Father, of the Son and of the Holy Ghost.*

Note that he says (name of) and not name. Father, Son, and Holy Ghost aren't names; they're titles.

Colossians 3: *And whatsoever ye do in word or deed, do all in the name of the Lord Jesus, giving thanks to God and the Father by him.*

Baptism is word and deed!!!

However I have one even better and this is apparently missed. Jesus said TEACHING all nations, baptizing them. If we were taught first it should end the controversy. Teaching must come before baptizing. However you must be willing to attend a church that's teaching truth in order to be accurately taught. Father (of Creation), Son (of Redemption) and Holy Ghost (of the Church) are best referred to as the Godhead.

Colossians 2: *For in him (Jesus) dwelleth all the fulness of the Godhead bodily.*

In today's society, you have to lock up and lock down everything. Many have numerous keys on their key ring. Therefore keys are very valuable. When you have someone's keys you have access to their home, car, office, in some cases even their church etc. Have you ever lost your keys? What was your first thought and action? After diligently searching with no avail, I believe you immediately began changing all your locks. Why? You didn't want anyone to use those keys and gain access to your valuables. If you have to retrieve something from a locked place, what's your first question? Where are the keys? What am I saying? If you want to enter a place, you have to go to the person that has the keys. Here's another important building block.

Matthew 16:13: *When Jesus came into the coasts of Caesare'a Phil'ippi, he asked his disciples, saying, Whom do men say that I, the Son of man, am? And they said, Some say that thou art John the Baptist; some, Eli'jah; and others, Jeremiah, or one of the prophets. He saith unto them, But whom say ye that I am? And Simon Peter answered and said, Thou art the Christ, the Son of the living God. And Jesus answered and said unto him, Blessed art thou, Simon Bar–jona: for flesh and blood hath not revealed it unto thee, but my Father which is in heaven. And I say also unto thee, That thou art Peter, and upon this rock I will build my church; and the gates of hell shall not prevail against it. And I will give unto thee the keys of the kingdom of heaven: and whatsoever thou shalt bind on earth shall be bound in heaven; and whatsoever thou shalt loose on earth shall be loosed in heaven.*

The above scripture details Jesus giving Peter the keys of the kingdom. I haven't found a scripture between Matthew 16 and Acts 2 where God requested or took those keys back.

Since Peter had those keys when the question *"Men and brethren what must be do to be saved?"* (Acts 2:37) was asked, he was the only one qualified and equipped to provide the answer.

If we are to compare Matthew 28:19 and Acts 2:38, you would have to recognize that there are distinct differences. Those distinct differences are the phrases "repent" and "remission of sins." The death of Jesus shows the extent that God would go to annihilate sin. His shed blood put our sins in remission.

Acts 2:38: *Then Peter said unto them, Repent, and be baptized every one of you in the name of Jesus Christ for the remission of sins, and ye shall receive the gift of the Holy Ghost.*

There are 22 New Testament references to the word Repent.

There are 25 New Testament references to the word Repentance.

Repentance is a required ingredient in God's plan of salvation.

Acts 2:39–42: *For the promise is unto you, and to your children, and to all that are afar off, even as many as the Lord our God shall call.*

God has to call you to this understanding.

And with many other words did he testify and exhort, saying Save yourselves from this untoward generation. Then they that gladly received his word were baptized;

Are you willing to GLADLY receive ALL the word of God?

And the same day there were added unto them three thousand souls. And they continued steadfastly in the apostles' doctrine and fellowship, and in breaking of bread and in prayers.

Acts 4:12:   Neither is there salvation in any other; for there is none other name under heaven given among men whereby we must be saved.

Let's look at a few other verses using this terminology:

Mark 1:4: *John did baptize in the wilderness, and preach the baptism of repentance for the remission of sins.*

Luke 3:3: *And he came into all the country about Jordan, preaching the baptism of repentance for the remission of sins;*

Luke 24:47: *And that repentance and remission of sins should be preached in his name among all nations beginning at Jerusalem.*

Acts 10:43: *To him give all the prophets witness, that through his name whosoever believeth in him shall receive remission of sins. .*

Without remission of sins, we could never be saved.

We say we love Jesus; so why debate about that.

John 14:13 & 14: *And whatsoever ye shall ask in my name, that will I do, that the Father may be glorified in the Son. If ye shall ask any thing in my name, I will do it.*

He gave us his name, Jesus, to use whenever we need it. When a person gives you their name they're giving you everything that they represent. It's equivalent to a blank check. I use his name for everything and I recognize that even in the natural, you don't get the benefits of using the name unless you have taken on that name in a formal ceremony. The exchange of marriage vows is a formal ceremony. Likewise the baptism in Jesus name is a formal ceremony.

I must be honest and admit that when I was first baptized in his name I didn't have the understanding that I now have. However, I had been going to Greater Emanuel and hearing truths I hadn't heard before. Those truths fed me even though I wasn't even a little bit spiritual at the time. I thank God for meeting me where I was and illus-

160

trating the principle to me in a way that I could understand. He showed me all the things I did, just in case. I'd purchased all types of apartment, car, health, and life insurance just in case. We purchase burglar alarms, and animals to protect us, just in case.

God knew my heart and that I didn't want to miss heaven. Therefore even though I didn't realize all the biblical truths I did understand the meaning in John 14:6: *Jesus saith unto him, I am the way, the truth, and the life: no man cometh unto the Father, but by me.* I knew that it was his blood that was shed. I walked down the aisle to receive my baptism. Down in Jesus name I went! Every time we baptize I'm reminded of the many sins that have been remissed in our baptismal pool.

Galatians 3:27: *For as many of you as have been baptized into Christ have put on Christ.*

I now know that to be the baptism in Jesus name.

Matthew 7:22 & 23: *Many will say to me in that day, Lord, Lord, have we not prophesied in thy name? and in thy name have cast out devils? and in thy name done many wonderful works? And then will I profess unto them, I never knew you: depart from me, ye that work iniquity.*

I heard Bishop say that's because they did everything but be baptized in his name.

11 Timothy 3: *All scripture is given by inspiration of God and is profitable for doctrine, for reproof, for correction, for*

instruction in righteousness. That the man of God may be perfect, thoroughly furnished unto ALL good works.

I'd like you to consider one last thought on this subject. We're still talking about those two scriptures in Matthew and Acts. One is inclusive and the other is exclusive. Hopefully, I've given you something to think about. If you seek him, he will reveal to you what you should do.

The bottom line for me is that I love Jesus and he died for me to be the best that I can be. I consider it an honor and a privilege to be baptized in his wonderful name.

Never thought I could be really happy and totally free
Ever since He came my way the sun is shining everyday
It's a good feeling; I am his and he is mine
To know he'll never leave; but he's with me all the time
Oh what a wonderful Change
since Jesus came into my life
Never will I be the same
since Jesus came into my life
Since he Came (A wonderful change)
Lisa Page Brooks

Father God,
Lord, the greatest thing about my life is you.
Bless this reader for their willingness to take the time to read about My Life Changed by Your Extraordinary Love. Please use this book to edify, encourage, and exhort, to provide laughter, produce tears, and to give this reader a greater understanding of your truths.

Lord, I thank you that you've made sure that your Holy Word was written and available for us. **PLEASE HELP US ALL TO BE THE ALL THAT YOU'VE PURPOSED US TO BE.**
(I pray that I've proven that I love you because I REALLY do!)

In Jesus Name,
Amen

My prayer for you is that you will seek him, regarding this and every biblical topic that concerns you. Salvation is very important. Please open your heart to him. Be willing to lay aside traditions, which hinder what God has purchased and purposed.

To order additional copies of

Have your credit card ready and call:

1-877-421-READ (7323)

or please visit our web site at
www.pleasantword.com

Also available at: www.amazon.com

Printed in the United States
26292LVS00001B/226

HOW DO THEY PACKAGE IT?

Westminster Press Books
by GEORGE SULLIVAN

How Do They Package It?
How Do They Find It?
How Does It Get There?
How Do They Build It?
How Do They Run It?
More How Do They Make It?
How Do They Grow It?
How Do They Make It?

HOW DO THEY PACKAGE IT?

by
GEORGE SULLIVAN

THE WESTMINSTER PRESS

Philadelphia

Book Design by Dorothy Alden Smith

Published by The Westminster Press®
Philadelphia, Pennsylvania

PRINTED IN THE UNITED STATES OF AMERICA

Library of Congress Cataloging in Publication Data

Sullivan, George, 1927–
  How do they package it?

  Bibliography: p.
  Includes index.
  SUMMARY: Traces the evolution of modern containers. Anecdotes about various packages such as the tea bag, consumption statistics, and environmental concerns are also included.
  1. Packaging—Juvenile literature. [1. Containers. 2. Packaging] I. Title.
TS195.S9   621.7′57   76–18089
ISBN 0–664–32601–3

CONTENTS

INTRODUCTION

IN FOOD PACKAGING, THE "GOOD OLD DAYS" WEREN'T SO good. Sugar, flour, and crackers were scooped out of barrels. Molasses and vinegar were drawn from kegs into bottles or jugs provided by the customer. Food was stored in unprotected bins, barrels, or sacks.

In the neighborhood drugstore, the pharmacist concocted his own cough syrups, toothache remedies, ointments, and laxatives. Hardware goods were sold in bulk, the storekeeper weighing out whatever quantity the customer wanted.

A revolution in sales and marketing techniques that swept the country around the turn of the century changed all this. Food and grocery products began to be packaged in individual containers—in paperboard cartons, metal cans, and glass bottles and jars.

That was only the beginning, however. The movement of people out of the cities and into the suburbs after World War II triggered golden days for the packaging industry. In the modern supermarket, with its approximately 25,000 different products, exciting packaging, commanding packaging, became as necessary as good lighting and check-out counters.

A package today plays many roles.

First it has to contain the product, hold its contents.

The package also has to protect. It has to protect against moisture and dirt, against extremes of heat and cold, and, in some cases, against the loss of flavor and fragrance.

Packaging is even used as means of protecting against pilferage. Take the case of ball-point pens. Were ball-point pens simply piled on the counter, they'd present an open invitation to the thief. It's an easy matter to slip a pen into one's pocket or purse. To prevent this, pens are blister-packed. Each is mounted on an oversize sheet of cardboard and covered by a clear-plastic bubble, a "blister." The cardboard is too big to fit into the shoplifter's pocket. Small toys and cassettes for tape recorders are other items that are blister-packed.

Lastly, the package has to communicate. This is frequently its most important role. The package has to tell the consumer the nature of its contents. It also has to announce the brand name, give instructions for the product's use, and perhaps even warn the consumer about the product's potentially hazardous nature. "The Surgeon General Has Determined that Cigarette Smoking Is Dangerous to Your Health," which is blazoned on every cigarette package, is the best known of such warnings.

In recent years, packaging's function has gone beyond these basic roles. There has been a growing demand for convenience food items, for individual dishes and whole meals that can be prepared in a matter of minutes. Often these products depend on clever packaging. Indeed, there are some food items available today which exist only because of the package. Those small cylinders of pre-mixed pastry dough to be found in supermarket refrigerator cases are one example.

Packaging today ranks as the most visible of all American industries. But its universality has led to a major problem—trash. What are communities supposed to do with all those discarded bottles, boxes, cans, and all the rest?

During the mid-1970's, the average American family discarded about 5.3 pounds of trash per day, and the

8

figure was getting larger year by year. It could reach ten pounds per family per day by the year 2000.

The trash problem has become so severe that legislation that would restrict the use of certain packages—"one-way" bottles, for example—or certain packaging materials has been considered in more than half the states.

No one wants to return to the days of the cracker barrel and the molasses jug. But no one doubts that food processors and container manufacturers could play a decisive role in reducing the great volume of trash each of us generates. They could, if they wanted to.

1

CRACKER BOX,
PACKAGING CLASSIC

THE MODERN AMERICAN SUPERMARKET IS A PACKAGING
wonderland. A hundred different types of aerosols await
the customer's push-button command. Metal cans in
brilliant colors offer the convenience of pull tabs or strip
tops. Gleaming glass bottles just need a twist to open.

Plastics have been molded into containers of inspired
forms, some of which rival sculpture in their beauty of
line. Yet, as bottles and jugs, they're easy to grip, easy to
hold.

But one of the best-known and distinctive packages
doesn't depend on modern technology or some space-age
material. It's a simple paperboard carton, not much
different today from what it was more than half a century
ago. It's printed along one side to represent a wheeled
circus cage with genial animals inside. At the carton top
there's a length of string attached by which the package
can be carried. It's the carton that contains Barnum's
Animals Crackers.

No one knows for sure who first thought of the idea of
baking and selling small cookies shaped like lions, tigers,
zebras, kangaroos, and a variety of other creatures. It's
believed that they were first imported from England at a
time when "fancy" baked goods were becoming popular in
America.

It is known that in 1878 two firms—Hetfield & Ducker
in Brooklyn and Vandeveer & Holmes Biscuit Company

11

To American youngsters this is one of the most famous of all packages

GEORGE SULLIVAN

in New York—were turning out "Animals," as they were called. The crackers were sold to grocers in boxes, barrels, or big glass-front metal cans.

Both of these New York bakeries eventually became part of the New York Biscuit Company. When this firm was merged with others to become the National Biscuit Company (now known as Nabisco), the name "Animals" was changed to "Barnum's Animals Crackers." Barnum was Phineas T. Barnum, a famous American showman of the day, and cofounder of the Barnum and Bailey Circus.

National Biscuit Company began selling the crackers in small paperboard cartons with the now-familiar circus-cage artwork in 1902. They appeared for the first time shortly before the Christmas season. A short length of string was fixed to the carton so it could be hung on the Christmas tree along with candy canes and strung popcorn.

It soon became apparent that Barnum's Animals Crackers were much more than a seasonal novelty. Indeed, within a few years after they had been introduced, they were well known in almost every American household.

In his book *The Philosopher Poet,* published in 1917, Christopher Morley wrote:

> Animal crackers, and cocoa to drink,
> That is the finest of suppers, I think;
> When I'm grown up and can have what I please
> I think I shall always insist upon these.

12

By the 1950's, Barnum's Animals Crackers not only were popular throughout the United States but were being exported to about seventy countries around the world. Five million pounds of crackers were being sold annually.

Through the years, there has been little change in the cookies themselves, and the basic design of the package has remained almost the same, a yellow package now being sold along with the original red one. What has changed is the manufacturing and packaging operations. They're a skillful blend of electronics, automation, and computer technology.

At Nabisco's giant biscuit and cracker plant in Fair Lawn, New Jersey, mixing and baking begin at one end and continue in a straight line to the other end. Raw materials and ingredients, stored in a 164-foot tower, are

In knocked-down form, cartons look like this

GEORGE SULLIVAN

13

Folded, glued cartons leave the package former

GEORGE SULLIVAN

delivered by automatic equipment to the mixing machines. Once mixed, the dough flows from a hopper to be flattened into a paper-thin sheet by two heavy rollers. After cutters stamp out the animals, they move on a conveyor belt through a band oven to be baked for approximately four and one-half minutes.

While the cookies are being formed, baked, and then cooled, the packaging operations are already under way. The cartons arrive from the Nabisco printing plant in knocked-down—flat—form. This makes it much easier to ship and store them.

They are delivered in huge sheets, with 32 box blanks on each sheet. Using a big pneumatic chisel, a workman divides the stacked sheets into piles of individual carton blanks.

The carton blanks are then fed into a package-forming machine. Metal fingers seize the blank at each end and fold it over a metal form which is the exact size and shape of the carton interior. The two ends are then glued together, forming a sleeve.

14

Cartons march in an endless stream to the filling machines

GEORGE SULLIVAN

At the same time, the four tabs that are to serve as the carton bottom are folded down and glued. The package-forming machine also attaches the string to each carton. Then, just before the carton leaves the package former, it is lined with waxed paper.

A conveyor system carries the cartons, open at the top, to the filling machines. Meanwhile, crackers are pouring from the bakery on conveyor belts into each of the filling

15

Four overhead conveyor systems feed crackers into filling machines
GEORGE SULLIVAN

Bundled cartons move on a conveyor system to the warehouse
GEORGE SULLIVAN

machines, in four streams. Each stream feeds a filling mechanism which automatically weighs the crackers, releasing just enough for an individual carton.

The cartons rush toward the filling machines, pause in groups of four to receive their allotment of crackers, then hurry onto other machines which close and seal the carton lids.

In the final step, the cartons are wrapped in brown paper in neat bundles, twenty-four cartons to a bundle. A label is affixed to each bundle. The bundles move on a conveyor belt to a storage warehouse to await shipment to supermarkets and other sales outlets.

Wherever they are sold, Barnum's Animals Crackers are almost always displayed and shelved fairly close to the floor. This is so that the cartons will be at about eye-level for children between the ages of two and six.

17

It's not only the colorful package and its circus theme that attracts youngsters. The string does too. It's an invitation to pick up the package, which few children can resist. "We wouldn't think of doing away with the string," says a Nabisco spokesman. "It's almost as much a part of the package as its distinctive size and shape."

.　.　.

In the packaging industry, it is acknowledged without question that the six-sided folding paperboard carton is number one. When it comes to the containing function that a package should have, no other type comes close to equaling paperboard.

Nearly every product we use is packaged in paperboard. The list includes milks and juices, cereals and baked goods, frozen foods and candy. According to the Paperboard Packaging Council, about 350 million paperboard packages are used every *day*.

Paperboard cartons are economical and easy to produce. They can be stored and displayed efficiently.

The folding carton is an excellent salesman, too, for it lends itself to the most sophisticated of modern printing techniques. It can be made as colorful and exciting as a magazine advertisement. Paperboard cutouts, such as toy airplanes or dolls, can be printed right onto the carton without any extra cost.

The paperboard carton is also available in countless shapes, sizes, and styles. A "window" can be cut into the carton front and covered with transparent film, thus satisfying the customer's curiosity about what the product inside looks like.

Almost all folding cartons are based upon one of two basic construction styles—tray style or tube style. The cigarette carton, which holds ten packages of cigarettes in two layers, is an example of the tray style. Soaps and detergents, cookies and crackers, are packaged in tube-style cartons.

Paperboard is different from ordinary paper in that it is

18

heavier, thicker, and more rigid. There are two types of paperboard. One is used in corrugated boxes and fiber boxes and is known as container board. The other type is used in making folding cartons. It is known as boxboard.

The first mill to manufacture paperboard was established in Milton, Massachusetts, in the early 1700's, but paperboard didn't begin to emerge as a packaging material until late in the following century. In 1879, Robert Gair, a Brooklyn, New York, printer and manufacturer of paper products, discovered methods for cutting and creasing cartons on printing presses. Gair converted several old presses into cutting and creasing machines. Later he began to illustrate his cartons, adding messages and designs by printing and embossing.

A giant step forward in the use of paperboard cartons was taken in 1899. That was the year that the National Biscuit Company introduced a new product, a flaky soda cracker named Uneeda Biscuit.

Crackers were almost always sold in bulk in those days, from barrels or big boxes. But officials of the National Biscuit Company wanted a new type of package, one that would prevent the crackers from getting moist and becoming stale. They designed a simple machine that enabled an operator to quickly form a paperboard carton from a flat

The modern version of the first stay-fresh package

GEORGE SULLIVAN

19

carton blank. At the same time he was forming the carton, the operator provided it with a waxed-paper lining. The carton also had a printed paper outer wrap.

When Uneeda packages first began to appear on grocers' shelves, they bore this message: "To protect, preserve and deliver to the consumer our new and splendid Uneeda Biscuit, as fresh and crisp as when just from the oven, we have devised this moisture proof package. Carefully remove the wrapper and after the biscuits are eaten, you have a school children's lunch box. Keep the box closed. This preserves the crispness."

The National Biscuit Company used newspapers, billboards, painted signs, magazines, theater programs, posters, window displays, and store banners to promote its new product. An enormous demand resulted. By 1900, sales for Uneeda Biscuit were averaging ten million packages a month, an undreamed-of figure.

Not only was the product an unqualified success in itself, but it signaled the beginning of a marketing revolution in food and grocery products. Bread and milk, butter and cheese, flour and rice, and coffee and tea began to move out of bulk barrels and boxes and into clean, neat, protective packages.

Following the success of Uneeda Biscuits, cereal manufacturers began using similar folding cartons. But whereas the Uneeda package bore printing on a separate overwrap, in the case of cereals the printing was done on the package itself.

Within the past two or three decades, paperboard cartons have become so much a part of our everyday life that we now take them for granted, like television and running water. But the widespread acceptance they eventually achieved was forecast more than half a century ago by the overnight success of Uneeda Biscuits and, of course, Barnum's Animals Crackers.

20

2
*PRE*PACKAGING

MODERN PACKAGING HAD LITTLE EFFECT UPON MOST FRESH fruits and vegetables until fairly recent times. They were usually shipped in bulk containers—boxes, barrels, baskets, or sacks—and sold in whatever quantity the housewife desired. She bought apples and potatoes by the pound, beets and carrots by the bunch (tops and all), and oranges and ears of corn by the dozen or half dozen.

That represented the traditional way such merchandise was marketed. In the earliest days of the country, farmers raised and consumed their own produce, and there was never any need to package it except for storage. If the farmer did want to sell any of what he grew, he hauled it to market in a horse-drawn cart, using any convenient barrel or box as a container.

The close packing, constant shaking, and lack of refrigeration caused rapid spoilage. The phrase "It takes only one rotten apple to spoil a barrel" was undoubtedly inspired by this kind of treatment.

Not until late in the nineteenth century was there any attempt made to retard the spoilage of fruit and vegetables intended for market through special packaging. In 1879, Australian orange growers began wrapping individual oranges in paper before shipping them to England. The practice became common in the decade that followed. American apple growers, who frequently shipped their product long distances, began paper-wrapping apples in

21

1895. It is said that the practice helped the apple industry develop a reputation for quality, bruise-free fruit.

The first attempts at prepacking fruits and vegetables turned out poorly. A New York City retailer tried selling potatoes in ten-pound and half-peck sacks in 1910, but the public looked askance at them.

Prepackaging of potatoes, and onions and oranges too, met with some success during the 1930's, but progress was slow. Tomatoes and spinach joined the list of prepack-

It takes only seconds to wrap a tray of oranges. Here, plastic film from a roll is drawn over trayed fruit

22

aged produce during the 1940's, and the trend continued with apples, celery, and citrus fruits during the 1950's. Still, the quantities involved were not large ones, and the traditional methods of retailing persisted.

The biggest strides in the prepackaging of fruits and vegetables were made during the 1960's. It was during this period that plastic film as packaging material came into widespread use.

Technically speaking, such wraps are known as thermo-

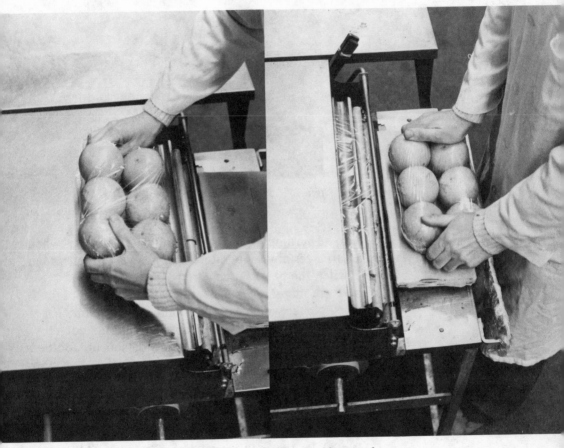

Ends are folded under the tray and package is placed on heat sealer. By pressing down on the contents, clerk seals package shut

GEORGE SULLIVAN

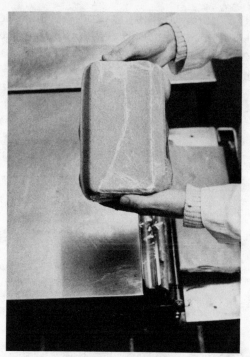

Seal is airtight

plastics. Thermoplastics are materials that melt when heated to a certain temperature but, like wax, they harden again when the heat source is removed.

There are many types of thermoplastics, including:

Polyethylene, which is lightweight, flexible, and has a waxlike feel. Often used as a wrapping material, polyethylene is also used in the manufacture of squeeze bottles.

Polypropylene is also lightweight and flexible, but more resistant to heat than polyethylene.

Polyvinyl chloride, often called PVC, is both strong and flexible. Besides its use in packaging materials, it is also used in the manufacture of phonograph records.

All of these thermoplastics are transparent. All have a sparkling appearance. They are available in sheets or rolls, in sleeves or bags.

24

In the wrapping of fruits and vegetables, plastic film is usually used in combination with small paperboard or plastic-foam trays. The trays are manufactured in a variety of sizes. One size holds four round pieces of fruit—oranges, for instance. Another size is just right for three ears of corn.

The tray containing the produce is covered with a sheet of plastic film. The ends of the sheet are then gathered together on the underside of the tray, sometimes so that they overlap one another. Then the tray is placed on a heated metal plate and pressed down on it. The heated plate melts the sheet plastic, causing the layers to fuse together and form a tight seal.

Some supermarkets wrap produce in what is called shrink film, which is a thermoplastic that has properties similar to that of a rubber band. Stretch a rubber band and it wants to snap back. Shrink film is the same. Heat, however, is what controls its ability to shrink.

The shrink film is stretched over the package of produce and it is heat-sealed. Then the package is placed on a

Package joins others on display

GEORGE SULLIVAN

25

conveyor belt and carried through a small tunnel wherein it is bathed in heated air. Although the package stays inside the tunnel only a second or two, the film is clinging tightly to the produce when it emerges.

Not all produce is prepacked at the supermarket. It may be done at almost any stage of the marketing system—at a central warehouse, a distribution terminal, or even in the field as soon as the product has been harvested. Tomatoes, carrots, celery, spinach, and cranberries are among the produce items packaged before reaching the point of sale.

While most fruits and vegetables are wrapped in thermoplastic and heat-sealed in the manner described above, there are several variations to the technique. The type of package used relates to the size of the item and whether it is a perishable product.

Retailers divide fruits and vegetables into five different classifications. They are soft fruit, hard fruit, stem produce, green vegetables, and root vegetables.

Soft fruits are highly perishable. Cherries, grapes, blueberries, strawberries, plums, and raspberries are considered soft fruits. "We don't even carry raspberries anymore," says one store owner. "No matter how carefully you handle them, they give you trouble. They bruise, they squash—and then they begin to rot."

Soft fruits are first packaged in small wooden, paperboard, or plastic boxes called "tills." They are then covered with film. But workers who do the packaging have to work carefully. The harsher the treatment these fruits receive, the shorter their shelf life.

Apples, oranges, peaches, and pears are hard fruits. They can take hard handling. Their shelf life is frequently measured in weeks, not days.

Hard fruits are usually packaged in an open tray or boat-shaped container, then wrapped in plastic film. Hard fruits can also be packaged in net bags or heavy-duty plastic bags.

Stem produce includes celery, rhubarb, and asparagus.

26

Cranberries are among the produce items that are packaged before they reach the retail level

GEORGE SULLIVAN

These are highly perishable because they lose moisture so rapidly. They have to be bagged or wrapped in moisture-proof film.

Green vegetables—lettuce, cabbage, broccoli, and cauliflower—quickly dry and wilt if not packaged properly. Like stem produce, green vegetables are usually wrapped in moistureproof film. But it's important that the package be ventilated; otherwise, spoilage begins.

Root vegetables have about the same keeping qualities as hard fruits. Typical root vegetables are carrots, turnips, radishes, onions, beets, and potatoes. They don't require delicate handling. They're capable of being stored for long periods.

Before root vegetables can be packaged, however, they must be washed, graded as to quality, and sorted by size. They are frequently packaged in heavy-duty plastic bags.

The plastic bags in which potatoes are packaged have an amber tint. This is to screen out light, which causes potatoes to start sprouting.

It must be said that prepackaging is not the only way in which to prevent fruit and vegetables from spoiling. Indeed, it is not even the foremost method. Temperature control is. Each fruit and vegetable has an ideal temperature for storage. If kept at this temperature, spoilage can

27

be delayed for days or weeks. And in some cases, apples or potatoes, for example, the delay can extend for many months.

What prepackaging does is prevent produce from losing moisture. All fruits and vegetables have an extremely high moisture content. It ranges from 70 to 95 percent. If left standing at room temperature, they quickly dry out. This causes wilting and shrinking. Bulk spinach, for instance, begins to wilt in a matter of hours. But when packaged in a bag of plastic film, spinach will retain its fresh appearance for days.

Prepackaging has many other advantages. Fruits and vegetables swathed in plastic wrap make for neater, more attractive displays, and this serves to stimulate sales. "We now get a lot of impulse buying in fruits and vegetables," says one store manager. "It's hard for a shopper to resist a box of strawberries or a tray of grapes in their glistening wrappers. They're mouth-watering."

Store managers also like the prepackaging idea because it makes for far greater efficiency. Since everything is weighed and priced in advance, each sale is accomplished in a much shorter period of time.

In addition, there's an advantage of flexibility. A store manager can adapt package sizes to meet local demands. "In the suburbs surrounding New York—on Long Island, for instance—our stores sell apples in ten-pound bags," the district manager for a large grocery chain explains. "But on New York City's East Side, where there are lots of unmarried people or families are small, our stores are likely to sell apples only four to a package. You seldom see apples in bags there."

There's less waste too. As one store manager recalls, "Customers used to 'pick over' and handle everything, and the produce suffered as a result. By the end of the day, just about everything had a tired look but the coconuts and eggplant. There were bushels of things we'd have to throw out.

"Well, that doesn't happen now. When customers

28

handle film-wrapped produce, it doesn't hurt its appearance."

Prepackaging has also helped to cut losses that resulted from pilferage. "We used to lose occasional apples and oranges, and people were always sampling grapes and cherries," another store manager recalls. "But not anymore. You can't make off with one apple anymore. You have to take a whole package of them—and that's a little bit awkward."

Since prepackaged produce is pretrimmed, there's a saving in shipping costs. Carrot tops and beet tops are removed in the field. The same with the outer lettuce leaves and cauliflower jackets. It used to be that these were shipped right along with the product, and it was the housewife who had to do the trimming.

One disadvantage of prepackaging can be the cost—that is, the cost of the package and the labor involved may be high in relation to the cost of the product. Bean sprouts are one example. When purchased in bulk, bean sprouts cost no more than twenty or thirty cents a pound. The prepackaged price is always two or three times that amount.

Another drawback is that it is impossible for the retailer to make up packages in sizes that suit every customer. A shopper might want to buy only one onion, but finds that the retailer has onions available only in packages of four or five. Or an economy-minded customer may wish to purchase potatoes or apples by the bushel, and finds they're being sold only in much smaller quantities. In both cases, a dissatisfied customer is probably the result.

Still another disadvantage is that some customers prefer to personally select their own fruit and vegetables, going through a bin or a crate and picking out just the pieces they want. "Those people are doing their shopping at the greengrocer's now," says the manager of a big supermarket.

The advantages of prepackaging far outweigh the shortcomings, however. Evidence of this is that year by year

29

produce retailers are becoming increasingly creative in their use of prepackaging techniques. It's now possible to buy prepackaged vegetables for soups or stews in the produce section of most supermarkets. Precut green beans, sliced melons, and peeled winter squash are other recent innovations.

What about the future? Melon balls and sliced tomatoes are being considered as prepackaged items. And citrus salads and prepared coleslaw. And even chop suey mix. The produce retailer has, quite obviously, come a long way from the apple barrel.

3

HOW DO THEY CLOSE IT?

WHATEVER A GLASS BOTTLE OR JAR CONTAINS, ITS FRESH-
ness to a great extent depends upon the container's
closure, the part of the package that forms its protective
seal. The search for reliable closures, which not only seal
tightly but unseal easily, dates to the earliest of times.

Among ancient Egyptians, one practice was to roll up a
strip of linen into a tight cylinder and use it to plug the
mouth of a jug. The linen cylinder was then sealed with
pitch.

Widemouthed earthenware jars containing wine were
sealed by pouring honey or oil over the wine, thereby
keeping the air out. Small glass vials were closed with
beeswax.

Cork became available to the Romans and Greeks as
early as 600 B.C. But corks did not come into general use
until much later, in the seventeenth century. There were
both straight and tapered corks, the wide end of the
tapered cork protruding from the bottle to be drawn out.

Cork is the bark of a kind of oak that is common to
most Mediterranean countries. Most of the corks used in
the United States and Canada come from Portugal. Spain,
France, Italy, and some North African countries also
produce cork.

It takes a young cork oak about thirty years to produce
its first usable cork. The cork is the bark of the tree, made
thick by nature to protect the tree from the intense heat of

31

Straight and tapered corks

GLASS CONTAINER MANUFACTURERS INSTITUTE

the Mediterranean summer.

There is an inner layer of live cork and an outer layer, the one from which corks and other cork products are made. It takes a skilled and experienced worker to remove the outer layer without damaging the inner one.

Bottle cork is boiled, flattened, and cut into strips. Machines punch out corks from the strips. Sorters then divide the corks into grades, the best being the least porous.

Cork is particularly well suited for closing wine bottles. One half of a cork's volume is air, held in tiny, watertight, airtight pockets. The average wine cork contains some three hundred million of these pockets.

When the cork is fitted into the bottle neck, the pockets along the cork sides are formed into millions of minute suction cups, thus making a perfect seal between the air and the wine. Cork also has the advantage of imparting neither odor nor taste to the bottle's contents.

When cork-based platform shoes came into fashion in the 1970's, it created an increased demand for the product. Cork prices went higher and higher. Wine makers reacted by reducing the size of bottle corks. At one time, fine wines produced in the regions around Bordeaux, France, were never stoppered with anything smaller than a two-inch cork. In recent years, however, corks that are

A wired-down stopper

GLASS CONTAINER MANUFACTURERS INSTITUTE

Codd's ball stopper

one-and-three-quarter inches in length have come into general use.

Corks were also tried with carbonated beverages, but they were not very successful. With beer, a tapered cork was first used, similar to what had worked so well on wine and whiskey bottles. But the beer cork, because of the gas pressure from within the bottle, had to be wired down to the bottle neck. Obviously, there was little that was quick or easy about such a system.

The first bottled soft drinks also relied on cork stoppers. The term "soda *pop*" is evidence of this. In describing soda water in 1812, English poet Robert Southey called it pop "because 'pop goes the cork' when it is drawn."

During the latter part of the nineteenth century, soda water, or pop, mushroomed in popularity in both England and the United States, and the search for a stopper more practical than the cork grew more determined. Many types of closures were introduced. The Codd bottle, the invention of Hiram Codd, an Englishman, was one. Patented in the United States in 1873, the Codd system was based upon a small glass ball that was contained within the bottle neck. Gas pressure from the beverage forced the glass ball against a ring of cork or rubber which was fixed inside the bottle neck, thus creating an airtight seal. In order to drink the beverage, one had to first stick a finger into the bottle and dislodge the ball.

The Codd bottle had to be filled upside down, which required a special filling machine. One advantage of the bottle was that it could be reused. But not many were. Young boys would frequently break the bottles in order to get the treasured glass marbles.

More successful than Codd's ball stopper was a closing

33

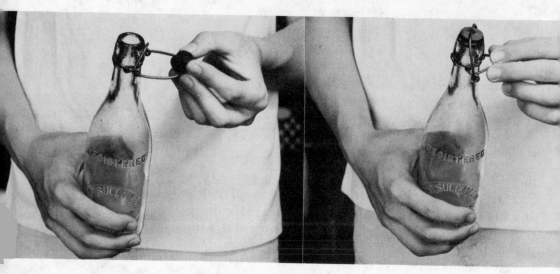

Lightning stopper was clamped into bottle neck, then tightened down by means of wire loop

GEORGE SULLIVAN

device known as the lightning stopper. This consisted of a vulcanized rubber stopper, centered on a loop of strong wire, and which could be lifted out of a bottle or clamped into it with the flick of a second wire loop which was fixed to the first. While the lightning stopper was not an inexpensive device, the fact that the bottle could be used again and again helped to defray its cost.

But a greater disadvantage than the cost was the health problem presented by these internal stoppers, as they were called. Bottles equipped with the lightning stopper or the Codd glass marble were difficult to wash. And the sealing device itself often served as a collection point for bacteria.

The problem was solved once and for all in 1892, the year William Painter, the foreman of a Baltimore machine shop, was issued a patent for a "bottle sealing device." It consisted of a small metal cap that could be crimped into a locking position on the bottle top. Its name: the bottle cap.

The bottle cap that Painter invented is very similar to

34

The bottle cap was a significant breakthrough

GEORGE SULLIVAN

the one in use today. The inner lid of the cap was fitted with a liner, a thin disk of packing material, which was critical to the cap's function. Painter suggested the use of cork liners. When the cap was locked to the bottle top, the liner formed an airtight seal across the bottle's mouth.

Surprisingly, bottlers of soft drinks and beer were slow to accept Painter's bottle cap. The device required the purchase of bottling machines and the expense involved in distributing openers so that consumers could get the cap off. A national depression in 1893 curtailed the availability of money for investment.

Another drawback was that bottles of the day were frequently handmade. Thus, bottle tops were scarcely uniform, and so bottle caps didn't always fit securely.

Michael J. Owens invented a fully automatic machine that turned out bottles (or jars) of uniform size in 1903. Only then did the use of bottle caps become widespread.

35

In the years that followed, high-speed, continuous automatic capping machines were developed.

The development of closures for jars and other widemouthed containers paralleled that of bottle stoppers, in fact, fruit jars of the early 1800's sometimes resembled tall bottles. To cap one of these, a housewife might wrap a corncob in a strip of cloth, then stuff it into the jar mouth. Later, when widemouthed jars became more common, a layer of wax or lard was used to protect the jar's contents.

But none of these methods represented a practical solution to the problem. It took the ingenious mind of one John L. Mason to develop a sure and simple method of sealing a fruit jar.

In 1858, at the age of twenty-six, Mason was granted

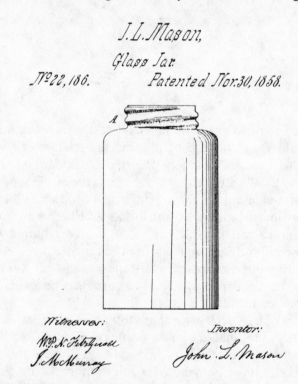

Patent drawing for the Mason jar

GLASS CONTAINER MANUFACTURERS INSTITUTE

patents for a screw-top jar, one in which the diagonal threads began just below the jar top and ended just before reaching the jar shoulder. When the zinc cap was screwed down, its rim came in contact with a thin rubber ring which encircled the neck and rested on the shoulder. By tightening down the cap, one achieved an airtight seal.

With the invention of the Mason jar, home canning became a reality. By the turn of the century, shelves in millions of American homes were well stocked with home-canned foods in Mason jars.

A rival to the Mason jar arrived in 1882, the invention of Henry W. Putnam. Putnam devised a system of clamping the glass lid to the jar rim by means of a short wire bail or yoke. The yoke was first fitted into a groove in the jar cover. By then pressing a hoop-shaped lever that was linked to the yoke, one tightened the cover against a rubber ring around the jar's neck. "When the lever is raised against the vessel," wrote Putnam, "the yoke will hold the cover loosely in position, and when depressed will hold it tightly."

Women of the day liked the lever feature because it made canning easier. During the processing, the cover could be kept loose. When the jar had cooled, the lever was snapped down. And the tightening of the seal was something a woman could do by herself. In the case of a screw-top Mason jar, it was usual for a woman to have to leave the top loose until the man of the house came home at night to give his strength to the final closing.

Jars with Putnam-type closures were called "lightning jars," because of their ease of operation. Mason jars were later provided with a clamp closure which was similar.

Screw closures for bottles followed in the wake of the development and widespread use of the Mason jar. But a problem developed with screw closures because each of the various glass container manufacturers had his own idea of what the pitch, length, and thickness of the screw threads should be. Not until the 1920's did manufacturers decide upon industry-wide specifications for screw caps.

For pull tabs, the future is not bright

GEORGE SULLIVAN

Only then did the caps come into universal use.

During the 1950's, with the introduction of the aluminum can, beverages in cans began supplanting beverages in bottles. The first cans of carbonated soft drinks did not have closures. The can ends were sealed shut, like a can of peaches or beets. To get the beverage out of the can, one had to use a special opener that cut a triangular shaped opening in the can top.

During the 1960's, cans with sealed ends were replaced by flip-top cans. These featured a removable pull tab. Before the decade ended, virtually every soft drink can in America was equipped with a flip top.

Manufacturers, and the public too, believed that the pull tab was the perfect method for opening a metal can. It was a cinch to use. It eliminated the need for an opener.

But it did lead to a glaring problem. Within a few years

38

Screw top bottles are in vogue today

after the device was introduced, pull rings and the small metal tab attached littered the country by the billions. Environmentalists began to cry out against their continued use.

The packaging industry reacted by developing alternative types of easy-open devices, ones that do not cause a litter problem. Several industry leaders have predicted that the pull tab will have all but disappeared by the beginning of the 1980's.

39

Thermoplastic caps often complement bottle labels in color and style

OWENS-ILLINOIS, INC.

One replacement is the strip-top can. In this, a nonmetallic tape is peeled back to allow the drink to pour through several small openings.

Then there is the button-top can. The consumer pushes a small lid to first relieve pressure inside the can. Then he pushes in a bigger lid to open a drinking hole. Both lids stay inside the can.

Other types of easy-open devices are also being tested. In the not too distant future, the flip-top can with the removable metal pull tab may have gone the way of the tinfoil tea package and the hand-blown glass bottle.

With closures, like packages themselves, there's been much more of a stress on convenience in recent years. Bottles and jars now boast a wide range of resealable tinplate and aluminum caps, and it doesn't matter whether the container is wide-mouthed or narrow-necked.

Thermoplastics (see Chapter 2) have also contributed to the modern look in closures. Polypropylene and polyethylene caps are to be found in myriad colors, shapes, and sizes, and frequently they're designed to complement the package label.

Despite all that's new, the wine cork carries on. Besides its ability to form a tight seal, cork imparts a certain elegance, a sense of refinement. Fine champagne in a screw-top bottle? It's unthinkable. There's no doubt that the cork, a standby for centuries, will be in use for many decades to come.

4

MAKING MILK SAFE

MILK HAS BEEN ONE OF MANKIND'S MOST HIGHLY PRAISED foods since Biblical times and even before. The Promised Land of the Israelites was said to be "a good and broad land, a land flowing with milk and honey" (Ex. 3:8).

But it is only in the past century or so that milk became completely safe to drink. As recently as 1901, William Thompson Sedgwick, a noted American biologist, could write, "Clothed in a veil of white, associated with the innocence of infancy, of high repute for easy digestibility, popular and cheap, milk has always deservedly held a high place in public esteem. Yet among all vehicles of infectious disease there is perhaps none more dangerous than milk."

Milk at the time was known to be the carrier of such infectious diseases as typhoid fever, diphtheria, and tuberculosis. In Great Britain it was commonly said, "Typhoid follows the milkman."

What happened, of course, was that milk processing and packaging methods went through a period of revolutionary change. In the years from 1860 to 1864, Louis Pasteur, a French chemist, demonstrated that by heating a foodstuff, usually a liquid, for a definite period of time at a specific temperature and then cooling it immediately, one could destroy the disease-producing bacteria that the foodstuff contained. But it took several decades before "pasteurization," as the process was called, came into widespread use in the United States.

Dr. Abraham Jacobi, a specialist in the diseases of children at the New York Medical College, observed the success of Pasteur's experiments while in Europe in 1860. The excellent results that Dr. Jacobi later obtained with the use of boiled milk in the prevention of diseases in children was noted by others, among them Nathan Straus. A merchant and philanthropist, Straus led the campaign for pasteurized milk in New York and, in 1893, established a number of depots where clean, heat-treated milk was made available to the poor.

While the contributions of Pasteur are well known, the history books have all but forgotten the pioneering efforts of one Gail Borden, an American inventor who was born in Norwich, New York, in 1801. Returning to the United States from England in 1851, Borden witnessed a shipboard tragedy that deeply affected him. Two cows had been brought on board to provide milk for infant passengers. During the voyage one of the cows became sick, and an infant died after being given the cow's milk.

Later, in both New York City and Washington, Borden witnessed other scenes that were reminiscent of what had happened on board ship. People often became sick after drinking home-delivered milk. Some died.

Milk dealers were unscrupulous in the way in which they handled the milk in those days. They added water to milk to increase its volume. They also doctored it with powdered chalk to make it whiter, then added molasses to give it a "creamy" texture. Some people of the day called it "swill milk."

Borden went to work to develop a process to preserve milk. Previously, he had been successful in preserving meat by drying strips of it, pounding it fine, and mixing it with melted fat to form a "meat biscuit." Borden believed that he had improved the keeping qualities of the meat by "condensing" it. Now, he reasoned, he would try the same process with milk.

He put a gallon of milk in a kettle and boiled off the

42

water until less than a quart remained. After it had cooled, he sipped some. The milk had a burned taste. It was very unpleasant. He knew that no one would ever buy it.

During a trip to New Lebanon, New York, not far from Albany, Borden visited a colony of Shakers, a religious sect that practiced communal living. He noticed that they condensed fruit juices and syrups by means of a vacuum pan.

The absence of air pressure permitted evaporation with less heat. The juices and syrups did not burn or discolor, and they had a pleasant flavor.

Borden borrowed one of the vacuum pans and returned to New York to try condensing milk again. After months of testing, he was able to produce milk that had no burned aftertaste and would stay fresh for several days before beginning to sour.

Borden, fifty-four years old at the time, was granted a patent for condensed milk on August 19, 1856. Two years later he opened a condensed-milk processing plant in Walcotville, Connecticut.

But the venture ended in financial ruin for him. When he began to produce condensed milk and deliver it to customers in New York City, the people rejected it. They were used to the taste of watered-down "swill milk." Pure and rich condensed milk tasted strange to them. Discouraged, Borden sold his interest in the company.

Borden tried again in 1858, a year that he and a partner, Jeremiah Milbank, founded the New York Condensed Milk Company. Borden's timing was better this time. Frank Leslie, editor of *Frank Leslie's Illustrated Newspaper,* an influential newspaper of the day, was waging a crusade against "swill milk."

When Borden had samples of his product ladled out from forty-quart cans, which were pushed around New York on handcarts, he found much greater acceptance for his product. By the end of the year, the New York Condensed Milk Company had invested in a horse and wagon and had begun serving a route of customers in Manhattan south of Fifty-first Street.

People soon realized that while both children and adults often became sick after drinking fresh milk, condensed milk could be consumed without fear. This was because Borden, in heating the milk to condense it, was killing off many of the harmful bacteria that the milk contained. In other words, Borden was unwittingly "pasteurizing" the milk, although it was to be several years before the discoveries of Louis Pasteur were made known.

Borden not only home-delivered condensed milk to housewives of the day, but also had it packaged in cans. Canned condensed milk, since it had excellent keeping qualities, could be shipped to any part of the world. Not long after the outbreak of the Civil War, the Federal Government ordered five hundred pounds of canned condensed milk. The Union troops liked it. Borden built several additional plants to keep up with the demand.

Condensed milk is a well-known supermarket product today. Frequently, the cans bear the Borden name.

.   .   .

Once milk pasteurization became standard practice and dairymen realized that the product had to be protected from contamination by dust and bacteria, the era of the glass milk bottle dawned. Bottled milk was available in stores, but usually it was home-delivered. Every day or, in some cases, every other day, the milkman brought milk to the homes of his customers and he picked up the empty bottles, which were sterilized and then refilled. The average glass milk bottle made about fifty such trips.

Early milk bottles were round and thick-walled and tapered to a wide mouth. They were sealed with a circular

A milk bottle of the 1880's

GLASS CONTAINER MANUFACTURERS INSTITUTE

Tank truck delivers milk into dairy processing system

paperboard cap which was sometimes covered with a tinfoil wrapper. In many areas, the round bottle eventually gave way to one that was squarer in shape, which saved space in the home refrigerator.

You don't see as many milk bottles anymore (although they are beginning to appear in antique shops and at flea markets). What happened was that milk packaging methods changed drastically during the 1950's and 1960's, a change triggered by increase in supermarket shopping. Filled glass bottles were much too heavy for the average

45

housewife to lug from the check-out counter to the family automobile. A lighter container was needed. Enter the paperboard carton.

Glass bottles are still used in the home delivery of milk, but they now account for only about ten percent of all milk sales. They are still in widespread use in some foreign countries, however. Bottled milk represents more than ninety percent of the market in England and Australia, and about sixty percent of milk sales in other European countries.

In Finland, interestingly, milk-bottle glass is tinted a dark brown, which works to filter out harmful light. Bottles of brown-tinted glass were once tested in the United States, but the American housewife would not accept them.

The first paperboard milk cartons were introduced just after World War II. The public liked the idea of the disposable container for milk. Empty milk bottles were a bother. They had to be washed, then stored until the milkman picked them up.

But there were some problems with paperboard cartons, and they did not win widespread acceptance. The first cartons were treated with wax to make them resistant to wetting. Often the wax would chip off, with the result that small wax particles would end up floating on the milk when it was served.

This problem was overcome with the introduction of polyethylene-coated paperboard cartons. Today, about two thirds of all the milk sold in the United States is packaged in cartons of this type.

Supermarkets stock mostly one-quart and two-quart sizes. Gallon cartons are seen frequently too, but as most shoppers know they have a tendency to leak.

This tendency led to the development of the one-gallon plastic milk jug. It's light in weight yet rugged, and features what is known as a "molded-on" handle, which makes the container easy to grasp. Because of its ruggedness, the all-plastic container is recognized as being

46

superior to the paperboard carton. But it is more expensive than the paperboard container, and thus not practical for use in the one-quart size.

Cleanliness keynotes every stage of milk processing and packaging. The procedure begins when milk is drawn from the cow's udder canals by automatic milking machines and piped directly through clear plastic tubing to the dairy farmer's storage tank to await transportation to the processing plant. The milk is kept refrigerated at from 40° to 50° F. It does not remain in the storage tank for more than a day or two.

Then the huge stainless-steel road tanker, often capable of holding up to five thousand gallons of milk, arrives and the farmer's supply is pumped into it. The milk is sold to the processor on the basis of weight, with the farmer receiving a fixed amount for each pound.

Milk used to be transported in ten-gallon milk cans, and some small dairy farms still ship milk in these containers. But the big tank truck represents the usual method of getting the milk to the processing plant. Once it arrives there, the milk is pumped into huge refrigerated vats where it undergoes testing to determine its fat content.

Inevitably there is foreign matter in the milk—body cells from the cow's udder, for example—and these have to be removed. This cleansing process involves a machine known as a centrifugal classifier, which spin-cleans the milk in much the same way a drier spin-dries one's laundry. As the milk is whirled about, the centrifugal force serves to separate the foreign matter from the milk itself. Even some bacteria is drawn off.

Now the milk is ready for pasteurization, not a complicated process. It consists of raising the temperature of the milk to 145° F and keeping it there for thirty minutes. However, many dairies now use flash pasteurization, wherein the milk is heated to a very high temperature (191° F, in some cases) and kept there for a very short time (less than one full second). Afterward, samples are tested to be sure the pasteurization has been effective.

47

In days past, when a bottled quart of milk was left standing for a few hours, fat globules in the milk, being light in weight, would rise to the top of the bottle and accumulate in the neck, forming a yellowish column several inches in height. This was cream. The bottle would have to be shaken vigorously before the milk was served in order to recirculate the globules of fat, or the cream might be skimmed off.

This isn't necessary today because milk is homogenized, a processing step that follows pasteurization. When the milk is homogenized, the fat globules it contains are reduced in size. They become evenly distributed throughout the milk and will not rise to the top. Homogenized milk is much easier to digest. But it also means that when

Automatic machines form cartons from precut, knocked-down blanks

GEORGE SULLIVAN

48

GEORGE SULLIVAN

a housewife needs cream, she has to purchase it separately.

After the milk is homogenized, it is ready to be packaged. There are many styles of paperboard containers in use throughout the United States, but the most common is the tall, rectangular package with the sealed gable top.

Cartons of this type are shipped to the processing plant in knocked-down form (as were the cartons for Barnum's Animals in Chapter 1). This saves space in shipping and storing.

Automatic machines form completed cartons out of the knocked-down blanks. Once formed, the cartons march on a conveyor belt to a circular filling machine. The filling machine revolves in merry-go-round fashion, with a dozen cartons "riding" at one time. As each empty carton boards the machine, a filled one leaves. After they are filled, another automatic machine seals the cartons.

During the mid-1970's the American dairy industry used paperboard cartons at the rate of about seventy million each day. But in other countries of the world, paperboard cartons are not nearly so popular. Milk is packaged in one-quart pouches in many European countries. In size and shape these pouches resemble the one-pound plastic-film pouches of beans and peas found in supermarkets.

Since a plastic-film package is cheaper than a paperboard container, there's an advantage in economy to the consumer. In addition, the pouch, since it lies flat, is easier to store. And it's easier to dispose of too.

A special, rigid plastic pitcher must be used to pour it. The pitcher holds the pouch upright and keeps the milk from spilling.

There's one other advantage that pouches have. It

49

stems from the manner in which they are formed and filled. In the milk processing plant, a roll of polyethylene film unwinds to form a tube that surrounds a metal filling pipe.

One end of the tube is sealed and then the milk flows in. Once the tube is filled, the other end is sealed. Now it's a pouch, a filled pouch.

The filling machine is equipped with ultraviolet lights. Directed at the film just before it is filled, they sterilize it. This means that milk will be free of many of the microorganisms that cause it to sour. It will stay fresh longer.

This advantage is more important in European countries than it is in the United States. An American householder is likely to purchase milk several times a week and store it in the refrigerator. But European adults and children consume less milk than their American counterparts. In addition, home refrigerators are not so common as they are in the United States. A French housewife, for example, is likely to store newly purchased milk in a kitchen cupboard for a long period before using it. Milk packed in a sterilized pouch permits her to do this.

Some American dairymen, milk retailers, and more than a few consumers have expressed dissatisfaction with the paperboard container. It is not the easiest package to open and reclose. In larger sizes, it can be difficult to handle. It has a tendency to leak.

Experts agree that the method by which milk is packaged is going to change. The milk container of the future may be a plastic bottle, a pouch, or perhaps some other type of container now being sketched on a designer's drawing board. Whatever develops, one day soon the paperboard carton is going to go the way of the home-delivered milk bottle.

50

5

A LITTLE SQUEEZE

THE 130-YEAR-OLD COLLAPSIBLE METAL TUBE IS ONE OF the most successful of all packages. Just about every American uses a tube at least once or twice a day, and sometimes much more frequently than that.

The reasons for the tube's success are easy to understand. It's the almost perfect package—airtight and lightproof, easy to use, a cinch to store, and economical.

The metal tube is also very versatile. About half of the one-and-one-half billion tubes sold annually throughout the world are used for toothpaste, but tubes are finding increasing use in the packaging of adhesives, cosmetics, hobby materials, and certain pharmaceuticals.

John Goffe Rand, a well-known American portrait painter of the nineteenth century, was the inventor of the collapsible metal tube. Born in Bedford, New Hampshire, in 1801, Rand went to Boston to study painting, and there became apprenticed to Samuel F. B. Morse. Morse, who later was to win renown as the inventor of the magnetic telegraph, was much admired as an artist.

As an apprentice, it was one of Rand's daily tasks to grind various paint pigments into powder. The powders were then mixed with water or oil to produce paint. If there was any paint left over at the end of the day, it was stored in a bag made from an animal bladder. The opening at the top of the bag was closed with a bone spike. But some air always managed to seep in, and as a result

51

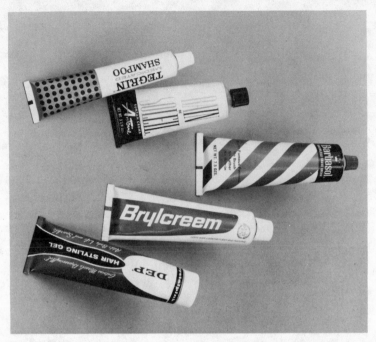

Metal tubes are used in packaging a variety of grooming aids
METAL TUBE PACKAGING COUNCIL OF NORTH AMERICA

the paint dried up. Since it was Rand who had to mix more paint, the problem concerned him more than anyone else. Not until he went to England in 1835 was he able to do much about it.

This was a period when the canning of food in metal containers was first becoming well established. Peter Durand, an Englishman, expanding upon the ideas first put forth by Nicolas Appert (Chapter 8), had demonstrated the practicality of preserving meats in tinplate canisters.

By the time Rand arrived in England, these canisters were well known, and it is not unlikely that they gave him the idea for the collapsible metal tube. In patents Rand received in the United States in 1841, he explained that his tubes were made from the same "drawn thin tin" as were canisters of the day.

52

Rand described his first tubes as being "metallic vessels so constructed as to collapse with slight pressure and thus force out the paint or fluid contained therein through proper openings . . . and which openings may be afterward closed air-tight, thus preserving the paint or other fluid remaining in the vessel from being injuriously acted upon by the atmosphere."

While Rand's early tubes were no different in theory than tubes of the present day, they were quite primitive from an operational standpoint. They were simply hollow cylinders, both ends of which were crimped shut. There was no neck, no opening for the fluid to flow through. To extract the paint, one punched a hole in a tube end. The hole was closed with a pair of pincers or by the use of metal solder.

Rand later developed tubes of improved design. A shoulder was formed at one end and fitted with an opening, and with what Rand referred to as a "nozzle."

In time, Rand's tube business grew prosperous, but he poured his profits into another venture, the manufacture of a device that could make a piano sound like an organ. When that undertaking failed and creditors began howling for payment, Rand was forced to sell the rights to his collapsible metal tube.

Rand died in 1873 and was buried in Woodlawn Cemetery in the borough of the Bronx in New York City. An artist's palette and a collapsible metal tube were chiseled onto his tombstone.

Tubes for artists' paints became well known throughout the world, although at first they were hooted at by art critics as being no more than a fad. Up until 1870, however, all metal tubes were made in Europe. That year a Philadelphia firm began manufacturing tubes for the American market. Before the century ended, several other companies in the United States were involved in tube manufacture.

Although tubes manufactured in Europe were used to package several other products besides artists' paints, this

53

was not true in the United States. But this situation began to change in 1892 when a New London, Connecticut, dentist, a Dr. Wentworth Sheffield, saw a new use for tubes.

Toothbrushing habits of the day were not noted for being especially sanitary. The family toothpaste was packaged in a small porcelain jar, and in using it each family member would dip his or her brush into the jar, taking the amount needed.

Dr. Sheffield realized that toothpaste packaged in a tube would have enormous advantages over the communal jar. Toothbrushing would be much more sanitary, for one thing. And because the tube was airtight, the paste would not dry out, which often happened in the case of the jar. Also, if dropped, the tube would not shatter.

Dr. Sheffield began importing metal tubes from Europe and filling them with a toothpaste he dispensed, a product he called "Creme Dentifrice." The demand was so great that Dr. Sheffield purchased a machine to make his own tubes. He began selling tubes too, and eventually the tube business proved more successful than selling dentifrice. In 1900, Dr. Sheffield formed the New England Collapsible Tube Company, which later became the Sheffield Tube Corporation. With headquarters in New London, Connecticut, the firm is still in operation.

The Colgate Company enjoyed extraordinary success with metal tubes. Founded in 1873, Colgate produced and sold dentifrices in powder, paste, and cake form, but not with great success. Colgate began using tubes in 1896. So great was the demand that within a few years the company ranked as one of the world's largest toothpaste manufacturers.

Colgate's first tubes were made of pure tin and had paste-on labels. But later the company adopted lacquered tubes upon which the company name and advertising slogans could be printed.

In 1908, Colgate introduced a tube with a special opening that dispensed toothpaste in a continuous narrow

54

strip, and proudly proclaimed the debut of "Ribbon Dental Cream." In full-page newspaper advertisements Colgate declared, "We couldn't improve the product, so we improved the tube."

It wasn't long before tubes began to be used for other products besides dentifrices and artists' paints. During World War I a Baltimore pharmaceutical firm developed a small collapsible metal tube with a shortened hypodermic needle fitted to the neck. Called a syrette, it contained a single dose of morphine, a pain-killing drug. Later, tubes of this type were used to dispense a variety of other medicinals.

The metal tube industry expanded rapidly in the years following World War I. Besides being used for several different brands of toothpaste by this time, tubes were used for a variety of soap products, creams, flavoring extracts, pastes, and glues. Tube designs had improved, and tubes of different sizes had been introduced.

World War II nearly crippled the metal tube industry. Almost 70 percent of all tubes contained tin at the time, a metal that became critically short in supply during the

A toothpaste tube of half a century ago (upright) *and a modern tube*
METAL TUBE PACKAGING COUNCIL OF NORTH AMERICA

55

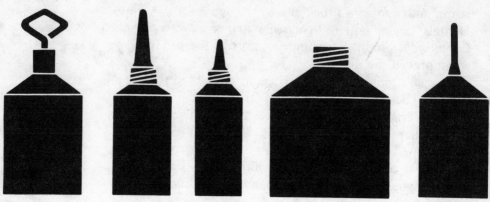

Tubes today are available in a wide range of sizes and styles, and with countless different types of openings

METAL TUBE PACKAGING COUNCIL OF NORTH AMERICA

war. To avoid virtual extinction, the tube industry organized the Tin Salvage Institute to collect scrap tin for use as directed by the Government. One of the Institute's regulations stated that no drugstore or supermarket could sell a tube of toothpaste without getting from the customer a used tube in return. The regulation thus helped to make tin collectors out of millions upon millions of Americans.

Once World War II was over, and the supply of tin and other critical metals stabilized, the metal tube industry enjoyed another period of mushrooming growth. Indeed, over the next two decades the production of metal tubes doubled.

At the same time the market was changing in size, it was also changing in character. For example, when shaving cream was introduced in 1915, much of it was packaged in metal tubes. Then, during the 1940's, the electric shaver was introduced, and millions of men stopped using shaving creams.

But the loss of this market was scarcely noted by the metal-tube industry, for tubes were being increasingly used for the packaging of such medicinals as antihistamines, antibiotics, and sulfa drugs. One metal tube out of every four was being used by the pharmaceutical industry

56

by 1968. The cosmetics industry also increased its use of metal tubes. Dentifrices, however, continued to account for fifty percent of all tube sales.

Not only is there a wide array of tube shapes and sizes, but tubes are fitted with many different tops and caps. For decades, the cap for the toothpaste tube was very small,

This tube's thin, tapered hollow tip is used as an applicator
METAL TUBE PACKAGING COUNCIL OF NORTH AMERICA

57

not much bigger than the crown of a watch stem. It was always getting lost, frequently being dropped and disappearing down the sink drain. Nowadays, the tube cap is long and tapered, and not easy to lose.

Some tubes, particularly those used for household cements, have a screw-eye opening. This type of cap prevents the adhesive from clogging shut the tube opening.

Tubes used for medicinal ointments often have a thin, tapered hollow tip. This aids in pointing the tube and applying the medicine to a specific place—into an eye to treat an infection, for example. What's called a "break-off" cap is used on tubes that contain a single medicine dosage. The tube remains sealed until opened, but cannot be resealed.

During the 1960's a dentifrice manufacturer introduced a toothpaste called Stripe. It came out of the tube striped like a peppermint stick. Its secret was a small, circular collar of red toothpaste built into the tube neck. The tube body contained white toothpaste. When the tube was squeezed and the white toothpaste flowed out, five thin strips of red toothpaste were deposited on it.

Caps on metal tubes used to be almost exclusively screw caps. But friction caps, which stay tightly in place after having been pressed onto the tube top, are very common today.

One fairly recent innovation is the oversize "stand-up cap." It permits a person to store a tube in an upright position, which saves on shelf space.

Tubes are manufactured from three different metals today: aluminum, tin, and lead. Aluminum is the most commonly used metal. Tubes for the packaging of most toothpastes, shaving creams, and cosmetics are made of aluminum. Because it is light in weight, aluminum reduces shipping costs. It is also strong and attractive.

But aluminum cannot be used with certain products because it reacts chemically with them, and this can serve to contaminate the product. Fluoride toothpastes are one example. When brought in contact with aluminum, the

58

Tubes that stand upright are a recent innovation
METAL TUBE PACKAGING COUNCIL OF NORTH AMERICA

product undergoes a chemical change. Fluoride toothpastes must be packaged in tin tubes, or in aluminum tubes whose inside walls have been treated with a special lacquer.

Pharmaceuticals are usually packaged in tubes of tin, while artists' paints, duplicating inks, and some hair creams appear in lead tubes.

The tube manufacturing process begins with small metal disks which vary in size from a dime to a silver dollar, depending on the size of the tube to be made. These disks are fed one by one into a die of a huge press. The die is a metal block which has a cylinder-shaped opening through

59

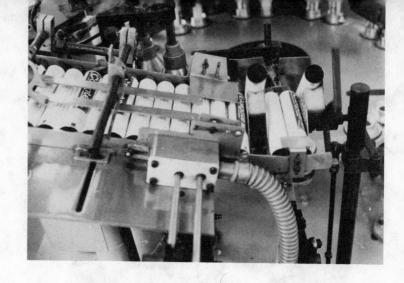

Capped metal tubes, open at the bottom, feed onto circular filling wheel

Tubes move into position under filling nozzles

Nozzles are inserted into tube bottoms and filling begins

Tubes wrapped in familiar cartons flow from packing machine

GEORGE SULLIVAN

61

the center. The opening is the same size as the tube that is to be formed. A metal disk fits into the top of the die. Pounding down on the disk comes the punch of a 200-ton press. The punch strikes the disk with such tremendous force that the disk metal flows into the cylinder, resulting in a form of tube shape. One end of the newly formed tube has a shoulder and a top. The other end of the tube is open.

This process is known as extrusion. After the tubes have been extruded, they are carried by a conveyor belt to a trimming machine which snips off the ends, making each tube exactly the right size. Next, the neck end of the tube is threaded, if the tube is to have a screw top.

The tubes are then coated with white enamel. To dry the enamel, the tubes are baked in a hot oven, after which the product maker's name and any design or advertising message he wants is applied.

This printed material has to go on to stay. To test the enamel, tube manufacturers will compress a tube back to almost the size of the original disk. Then they draw the tube open again. The tube may be a mass of wrinkles, but the paint will be unscratched and the advertising message undistorted.

After the tubes have been decorated, the caps are put on by automatic machines. As this implies, when the tubes are filled, they are filled from the bottom. After the caps are in place, the inner walls of the tubes may be lined with lacquer, wax, or some similar substance. Then the tubes are inspected, packaged, and shipped to product manufacturers.

Automatic machines fill and close toothpaste tubes at the rate of 100 to 300 per minute. Each tube is lifted onto a filling nozzle. When the nozzle tip has been inserted as far as the tube cap, the toothpaste is pumped in. As the filling continues, the tube is progressively lowered so that there will be no air spaces within the filled tube.

There are several methods of sealing shut the open ends of tubes. The standard method is to give the end a double

62

fold and then crimp it. Another method is to double over one fold inside the other, then crimp.

New products are being packaged in tubes all the time. Glazing putty, which is used to secure panes of glass into their frames, is now available in tubes. When the tube is squeezed, the putty oozes out in a triangular-shaped ribbon, making it easier to apply. Many caulking compounds, which are used to make seams watertight, are also packaged in tubes. When caulking a roof, for instance, the roofer can simply carry the tube or caulking compound in his pocket as he climbs the ladder. If he should accidentally drop the tube, it doesn't get damaged. Lubricants and ski wax, printing inks and fire-starting jelly, auto wax and other products are now available in tubes.

In Europe, many types of foods are packaged in metal tubes. Mustard is sold in tubes in England, as is tomato paste. In Switzerland, one can buy butter, cream cheese, honey, and chocolate syrup in tubes. It has been estimated that in some European countries about one half of the metal tubes produced are used in food packaging.

But food packaged in metal tubes has never won wide acceptance in the United States or Canada. This is true

In Europe, food in tubes is popular
METAL TUBE PACKAGING COUNCIL OF NORTH AMERICA

even though there are certain occasions when a collapsible "food tube" would be a most efficient package. A tube of ketchup or mustard on a picnic would seem to be very practical. The product would stay fresh. The package would be lighter in weight than a jar. There would be no worry about breaking it.

Tubes of cream cheese, mayonnaise, or cheese would be useful at home barbecues or in school lunches. Not only are tubes sanitary, but a knife or spoon wouldn't be needed to dispense the product. You'd just squeeze it on. Jelly and jam, cake frosting, chocolate sauce, and meat and fish spreads could be packaged in metal tubes.

The delights of having peanut butter packaged in a metal tube were summed up recently by one of the prizewinning entries in a contest to find new tube uses sponsored by *Boys' Life* magazine and the Metal Tube Packaging Council of North America. Submitted by a Jackson, Michigan, sixteen-year-old, it read:

> Peanut butter is my bag
> But sometimes not so neat!
> I'd love to get it in a tube
> For a TUBEr goober TREAT!
>
> I could carry it in my pocket
> And then with just a squeeze
> I could put it on a cracker—
> My snacks would be a breeze!
>
> A squeeze of peanut butter
> Would beat a spread by far.
> My Mom thinks it would beat the mess
> Of knives in pail or jar!

Such enthusiasm is not typical, it must be said. Americans and Canadians, in fact, have been slow to accept the idea of food in tubes. Why? "It's because," says a spokesman for the metal-tube industry, "they associate metal tubes with toothpaste, with cleaning the teeth. They have a psychological block about using the same type of container as a food package."

64

But more than a few industry experts believe that one day Americans and Canadians will come to realize the benefits of metal-tube packaging for certain foods, and that they will overcome their present distaste for tubes used this way. But nobody is saying it's going to happen next week.

6
BETTER BY DESIGN

IN THE DAYS THAT THE CORNER GROCERY STORE FLOUR-
ished, the housewife usually made her purchases on the
basis of past experience. She knew what brand of soap
had satisfied her in the past. The same with flour, salt,
coffee, and most other products.

But in cases where she was unsure, she would ask the
storekeeper to make a recommendation. "You'll like these
crackers, Mrs. Jones," he might say. "My wife is always
having me bring some home."

Then came self-service, and suddenly there was no
storekeeper upon whom the shopper could depend. The
man who manages the modern supermarket is usually too
busy to chat about any of the tens of thousands of
products he offers. The stock boys are seldom aware of a
product's merits or lack of them.

What has happened is that the package itself has
replaced the storekeeper as a salesman and source of
information. Of course, the package's basic roles are to
contain and protect the product. But it's just as important
that the package communicate—perhaps even more important.

The package must identify the product and give the
brand name. It must impart instructions for use, report
warnings that might be appropriate concerning the product, and present any guarantees or warranties. Most of all,
it has to sell itself, to say, "Hey, pick me!"

A playful design to remind mothers of their children

STEPHEN LION

Take the case of the paperboard cartons of fresh lemonade bearing the Sealtest name that are to be found in supermarket refrigerator cases everywhere. The carton features bright-yellow drawings of lemon slices. The drawings are very lighthearted in character.

"Mothers buy this product, but it's their youngsters who drink it," says Stephen Lion, the art and design consultant under whose direction the package was developed. "So we sought to attract mothers by representing the lemon in a playful manner, in a juvenile manner. This reminds the mothers of their youngsters at home. And, thinking of the youngsters, they buy the product.

"We also used a green background for the drawings of the lemon slices. Green to most people symbolizes health."

Stephen Lion heads a firm that specializes in package design. There are more than one hundred such firms in the New York City area alone.

In addition, large paper companies and manufacturers of plastic film and glass containers employ designers whose services are available to potential customers. For example, a cooky or cracker manufacturer can always get

67

Introduction of bottles with polystyrene wrappers made for major changes in design

OWENS-ILLINOIS, INC.

plenty of packaging advice from International Paper Company, Champion Paper Company, or any other firm making paperboard containers.

It's not just new products that require new packages. Sometimes there's a need to redesign the package of an existing product.

It may be that the product has been improved in some way. For example, the manufacturer of a laundry detergent may have added a special whitening agent to his product. Naturally, he would want to proclaim this improvement to potential customers. A newly designed package would be essential.

Sometimes packages get redesigned because of a change in the package itself. When soft drink manufacturers began to switch over to bottles with wraparound polystyrene sleeves, which could be preprinted and decorated in a

68

rainbow of different colors, revolutionary changes in design took place.

Sometimes a package will be redesigned simply to give the product a new look, a fresh face. It's a tried and proven method of reviving customer interest.

In developing a package, the designer begins with the physical characteristics of the product. How tall is it? How wide? How much does it weigh?

He has to know any special properties the package might have to have. Is spoilage a problem with the product? Must it be protected from extremes of heat? from moisture? Is it likely to mold? to rust?

He has to be aware whether the package has to have an easy-opening device, such as the spout on the cylinder-shaped salt box. He has to know how the package is going to be handled in the supermarket. Is it going to be stacked and shelved? Or is it going to go into bins?

It's important that the package have the capability of being unitized, that is, it must be of such a size and shape that it can be combined with other packages of its type so that it can be transported from one point to another in the marketing chain with the least possible labor and mechanical energy.

Take the case of an individually wrapped candy bar. Twenty-four bars are placed in a box; twelve boxes are placed in a shipping carton. The cartons are further unitized on a pallet for easy handling at the warehouse.

In some cases there is not much latitude for the designer. The size, shape, and character of the package are pretty much determined in advance. Bar soap is wrapped. Soap powder is boxed in paperboard containers of traditional size. The same holds true for dry cereals, cookies, baby food, and hundreds upon hundreds of other products.

Thus, most of the designer's creative talents go toward developing a package that will attract the buyer. He does this by the clever use of graphics, a term that refers to any words or pictorial images that appear. He also chooses

69

colors that are appropriate and distinctive.

Any symbols that might be part of the package design have to be selected with the greatest care. Most people like ovals and circles, but triangles are said to appeal only to men.

Package design of the present day must also include the product's Universal Product Code. Scanning equipment at the supermarket check-out counter "reads" the UPC symbols on the various packages, permitting clerks to total bills with lightning speed. The UPC system also aids the store manager in keeping his inventory up to date and in reordering.

Package design is also concerned with the manufacturer's trademark and distinctive name—the brand name. While it is true that virtually every grocery product sold today has its own brand name, the practice is not very old.

Branded products were little more than a novelty until the latter decades of the nineteenth century. When one went to a general store and purchased crackers, butter, molasses, coffee, or tea, a brand name was never asked for. If molasses was ordered, the storekeeper poured some molasses from his barrel into the customer's molasses jug. Tea was scooped out of another barrel, coffee beans out of still another. And so on.

In the years that followed the Civil War, the nation went through a period of great industrial and commercial growth. The nation's population expanded. The demand for goods was so great that people bought almost anything that was offered. But with the improvement in production facilities and transportation, the situation changed. A buyer's market was created. Competition developed.

There was also a change in marketing practices. The

THE "IVORY" is a Laundry Soap, with all the fine qualities of a choice Toilet Soap, and is 99 44-100 per cent. pure.

Ladies will find this Soap especially adapted for washing laces' 'nfants' clothing, silk hose, cleaning gloves, and all articles of fine texture and delicate color, and for the varied uses about the house that daily arise, requiring the use of soap that is above the ordinary in quality.

For the Bath, Toilet or Nursery, it 's preferred to most of the Soaps sold for toilet use, being purer and much more ple...nt and effective, and possessing all the desirable properties of the finest unadulterated White Castile Soap. The Ivory Soap will "float."

The cakes are so shaped that they may be used entire for general purposes, or divided with a stout thread (as illustrated into two perfectly formed cakes, of convenient size for toilet use.

The price, compared to the quality and the size of the cakes, makes it the cheapest Soap for everybody and every want. Try it. SOLD EVERYWHERE.

Ivory soap was one of the first brand-name products. This advertisement appeared in 1873 years after the Civil War saw the rise in importance of the chain store. The first big grocery chain, The Great Atlantic and Pacific Tea Company (the A&P today), had ninety-five stores in operation by 1880, scattered from Boston as far west as Milwaukee. Department stores became an important marketing factor, too.

These stores had the room to display many different products. They might feature three or four brands of soap, several different teas, and so on. For the first time, it became necessary to distinguish one brand from another.

There were only a handful of trademarks registered with the U.S. Patent Office in 1870. By the turn of the century, there were more than ten thousand registered names. Obviously, a revolution had taken place. Some of the best-known brand names of the early 1900's included Shredded Wheat, Grape Nuts, Regal Shoes, Ivory Soap, and Knox Gelatine.

In time, package designers found that the colors the package would feature had to be chosen with the utmost care. When a designer chooses a color, he realizes that he is dealing with human emotion. His choice can render the package, and thus the product it contains, exciting or dignified, whimsical or staid.

Red is packaging's all-purpose color. It makes a package look important, gives it a commanding appearance.

Red never fails to catch the eye. An executive of a major food-processing firm is said to have always instructed package designers with these words: "Give us any color as long as it's red."

Yellow gets high marks as an attention getter, too. In addition, yellow has a cheerful, vibrant look to it.

Blue is said to imply refinement. Many food packages

WARNING
KEEP OUT OF
REACH OF CHILDREN

SUGGESTED SERVING

These symbols and phrases appear frequently on packaged goods
NEW YORK PUBLIC LIBRARY

71

carry blue borders, which impart something of a prestige factor, like displaying a blue ribbon.

Blue also stands for cleanliness. Packages of soaps, detergents, and household cleansers often feature blue.

Green is extremely popular with package designers. It is a soothing color, the color of hope. "Green is a color of wide appeal; cool, fresh, and comforting in its beauty," says Faber Birren in his book *Your Color and Yourself.* "It is a sign of balance and normality. It has the universal appeal of nature."

Designers have much more freedom today in their choice of colors than they used to. It wasn't long ago that the cosmetic counter abounded in soft pinks, and packaged products for men featured dark browns and grays. That kind of thinking has gone the way of the iceman.

Cereal packages never fail to stress color and excitement

GEORGE SULLIVAN

There are no hard-and-fast rules. The package color must get attention and express the product's reliability. Any color or combination of colors that can achieve these goals is suitable.

There is one exception to what is stated above. Some corporations, through years of advertising and promotion, build a strong identification with a particular color. This color becomes the dominant one in the company's packaging. When one thinks of a Kodak product, yellow is the color that immediately comes to mind. Howard Johnson's will forever be identified with bright orange.

Lavoris' color is red, Listerine's is amber. Del Monte products feature green. And then there's the Green Giant.

When it comes to color, the designer has to find out how competitive products are being packaged. Perhaps one of the leading brands in the field features a blue box with gold trim and a bright color photograph of the product. Naturally, the designer will avoid any design that's similar. What he is likely to do instead is develop a contrasting design, one that will give his product a display advantage on retailers' shelves.

In the case of a product that is going to be sold in foreign markets, the designer has to realize that colors often have different meanings in different countries of the world. In the United States white is often used to signify purity or cleanliness. But in some Asian countries white is associated with mourning.

When an American manufacturer introduced his product in Hong Kong in a purple package, it stayed on the store shelves. Then it was learned that purple is considered an unlucky color to the Chinese. When the package color was changed to red, the product was immediately successful.

Not long ago an American company that sells canned tuna introduced its product in Japan. It failed miserably. After an investigation company officials learned that the product's failure stemmed from the package design. It featured the picture of a tuna swimming in the ocean waves, its head pointed downward. To the Japanese housewife a fish with its head down indicates a dead fish. As soon as the picture of the tuna was changed, sales perked up.

Sometimes there are federal regulations that mandate that certain information about the product must appear on the package exterior. This information may take the form of a warning. Keep Out of the Reach of Children, a bottle of medicine may say.

In recent years, the art of package design has reached new heights. Evidence of this is that there are certain products that exist today only because of their packages.

Those cylinders of biscuit dough to be found in the

Innovations in packaging design and engineering made these products possible

GEORGE SULLIVAN

74

refrigerator cases of the nation's supermarkets are recognized as being one of the modern triumphs in the field of food packaging. The dough they hold is completely mixed. It needs only to be removed from the package and baked for a short period.

Finding a package that would hold the dough was no easy matter. The dough was sticky and gummy, and since it contained baking powder it could easily expand if exposed to the slightest amount of heat. The package also had to be one that would store easily in a refrigerator case.

What is called a "composite container" was finally developed. It consists of a foil-lined paperboard cylinder with metal ends. The dough can't stick to the smooth and shiny foil. The walls of the container are made of several layers of board, spiral-wound for added strength and easy removal.

Or consider orange juice and the way in which it is marketed today. Up until the mid-1940's, the housewife who didn't want to be bothered squeezing fresh oranges had to serve canned orange juice. But canned orange juice had a flavor all its own, and it scarcely resembled the flavor of the fresh product. It tended to be thin and watery too. Canned orange juice was never very popular.

The next step was to freeze freshly squeezed juice and market it in that form, like frozen strawberries or green peas. But the product was never very successful in this state because it took so much time to thaw the juice. People do not have much time available at breakfast, when most orange juice is consumed.

Then processors and packagers decided to first concentrate the juice before freezing it. The concentrated juice was packaged in a lightweight six-ounce can, then frozen. To restore the juice to its original state, the consumer added three canfuls of water to the concentrate. The package was a measuring cup, in other words. The concentrated juice melted as it was being mixed. It was a simple operation. A young child could do it.

Best of all, frozen concentrated juice had much the same

75

taste and aroma as freshly squeezed juice. It was pure and safe.

The first frozen orange juice cans were all metal. A can opener had to be used to get the can open. Nowadays frozen orange juice is packaged in foil-lined paperboard cylinders or plastic containers. They usually feature tear-strip opening devices.

This packaging system contributes to the product's low cost. The processor ships only the juice, and that is in concentrated form. Shipping the oranges would mean shipping six times as much weight. And there's an environmental benefit too. The waste remains at the processing plant, where it is often sold as cattle feed. In the case of freshly squeezed oranges, the skins wind up as municipal refuse.

The success of frozen orange juice triggered the growth of an entire industry. Supermarket freezers are now filled with cylinders of frozen grapefruit juice, pineapple juice, lemonade, limeade, and many other fruit drinks.

As these paragraphs suggest, many products that exist

Success of frozen orange juice concentrate led to the development of countless other similar products

GEORGE SULLIVAN

76

Another triumph for modern packaging

GEORGE SULLIVAN

today by reason of package design are in the convenience-food field. The Snack Pack is another example. The term Snack Pack refers to the small cans of pudding and fruit used as desserts by people who carry their lunches to work or school.

There's really nothing unique about packaging pudding in a can. Food processors have had the ability to do this for about a century.

But what made Snack Pack practical was the development of the strip-top can. Pull a small ring mounted to the can top and you open the lid. It's as easy as opening a box of crackers.

Before the strip-top can was introduced, you had to use a can opener to open a can. No one was likely to carry around a can opener just to be able to enjoy pudding for dessert. It was easier to pack along an apple.

Many authorities in the field of package design believe that such innovations as the Snack Pack and those small

77

cylinders of frozen concentrated orange juice and pastry dough represent the wave of the future. American consumers are going to be seeing more and more new products in the years to come, but their newness will derive from the package more than any other factor.

7
A MATTER
OF CONVENIENCE

During World War II, an English war bride living
in the United States sent her mother in London a package
containing over two hundred tea bags. Since England, a
nation of tea lovers, was experiencing a severe tea shortage
at the time, the woman knew that her mother would be
cheered by the package.

Not long after the tea arrived, the woman received a
letter from her mother. "Thank you very much for the
tea," said the letter. "It was delicious. But it took an
awfully long time for us to get it out of all those little
packages."

The story, a true one, gives some insight into the way
American consumers take inventive packaging for
granted. In eliminating the guesswork that used to go into
the preparation of a "perfect" cup of tea, as well as doing
away with the bother of loose tea, the tea bag rates as one
of the best examples of today's popular convenience
packages.

It also happens to be one of the first. Through the
centuries, the accepted method of brewing tea called for
one to measure out loose tea in a teapot and cover it with
boiling water. The leaves then had to be allowed to
"steep," that is, soak. Steeping serves to release the
delicate flavor of the leaves into the water.

When the tea was poured from the teapot into one's
cup, some of the leaves went along. No one cared too

This tea "ball" has a teapot shape

GEORGE SULLIVAN

much about this. If you drank tea, the leaves were an inconvenience you learned to put up with.

Teapot makers sought to overcome the problem by making the tea pass through a perforated ceramic shield as it entered the spout. This strained out some of the leaves, but not all of them. If the perforations were made too small, the leaves clogged them and the tea would only dribble through. When the holes were made larger, they didn't stop any leaves at all.

Another solution, introduced during the nineteenth century, was the "tea ball," or "tea egg," as it was called in Europe. This was a metal ball made in two halves which were joined by a hinge. After the tea leaves were inserted in one half, the other half was folded over and the ball locked shut. A chain attached to the ball enabled the user to remove the ball from the cup after the tea had steeped. Such tea balls are still in use today, and can be purchased in most department stores and kitchenware shops.

A somewhat similar device, the perforated teaspoon, came later. This took the form of a conventional teaspoon, but was pierced with rows of small holes and fitted

80

with a lid of the same size and shape. You simply filled the spoon bowl with tea, closed the lid, locked it, and placed the spoon in the heated water of your cup.

At the same time, teapots were being introduced that featured perforated metal balls or baskets that rested on the pot bottom and were attached to the pot by a metal chain. American manufacturers introduced teapots in which the ball or basket could be raised or lowered by turning a knob which was built into the pot lid. When in a raised position, the ball fitted into the recessed area under the pot's curved lid. In another teapot of the day, the tea ball was attached to a timing device inside the pot lid which automatically raised the ball after a preset number of minutes.

But most tea drinkers, instead of using the elaborate pots and tea balls described above, preferred a simple tea strainer. Made of fine metal mesh, the strainer's size and shape was such that it could rest over the cup rim. You simply poured the tea from the pot through it.

One manufacturer sought to improve upon the strainer idea by designing a pot in which the strainer was attached to the spout. But the spout-strainer was messy because it dripped. It was to go the way of the buggy whip.

Enter the tea bag!

According to the Tea Council of the U.S.A., tea bags date to the year 1904. They were first created by Thomas Sullivan, a New York City tea and coffee merchant. Sullivan was planning to send a few samples of his tea to potential customers. It was usual in those days to send samples in small tins, but Sullivan decided it would be easier and less expensive to put the tea in small bags. He ordered hundreds of little silk, hand-sewn bags, filled them with tea, and sent them out to his customers.

He was wholly unprepared for what happened. When orders began coming in, they were not for tea in bulk quantities, but for more bagged tea. His customers had discovered that by pouring boiling water over the bags they could make tea with much less fuss.

Another twenty or thirty years went by before tea bags achieved widespread popularity. The Thomas J. Lipton Company introduced the tea bag as a branded, nationally advertised product to hotels and restaurants in 1919. Tea bags did not become available in grocery stores and supermarkets until 1929.

The first tea bags were, like Thomas Sullivan's, made of cloth, of an almost transparent fabric with a loose and open weave. It resembled gauze. Some of the early tea bags had a pouch shape. These consisted of a circular piece of cloth which, after it had been filled, was gathered at the top and tied with thread. Other tea bags of the 1920's were made in the form of tiny pillows. They could be square, oblong, or even round in shape. A string and tag were common to all types.

By the 1930's, there were about twenty American tea packers who owned tea-bag-making machines. These machines automatically cut the bag cloth to the proper size. Tea leaves from a rotating tube were fed onto an automatic scale. When the scale had received the required weight, it tilted to one side, depositing the tea onto the cut cloth. The cloth was then formed into a pouch and the neck tied. The string and tag were added. Such a machine could produce as many as eighteen thousand filled bags in an eight-hour day.

The tea bag today is not a bag at all, but a small packet of porous, wet-strength paper. It has become so popular that approximately one half of all tea consumed in the United States is packaged in tea bags.

. . .

The world's tea "belt" stretches from India to Ceylon, and from Indonesia to Africa. Tea is also grown in some South American countries.

After the leaves are picked, they are spread on trays to wither. They are then rolled, a process that liberates the leaf juices. It is these juices that give the tea its flavor. Next, the leaves are fermented and then dried.

As they emerge from the drier, leaves of different sizes, some broken, others unbroken, are all mixed together. They are passed through a series of sifters which sort them according to size.

A whole leaf is slow to release its color, aroma, and flavor. Broken leaves are much quicker to brew. They make for a stronger, darker tea than whole leaves. It's broken leaves that are used in tea bags.

One particular grade common to tea bags is broken orange pekoe (pronounced peck-o, not peek-o). The term orange pekoe refers to a leaf size and has nothing to do with quality or flavor. It is one of the smaller leaf sizes.

Broken orange pekoe is the smallest of the leaf grades. It produces a tea of good color and strength.

Broken pekoe is another grade used in tea bags. Broken pekoe leaves are slightly larger than broken orange pekoe, but they produce little color in the cup. They are used mostly as a filler rather than for flavor.

Tea experts recognize more than three thousand different varieties of teas. Within each variety, quality can vary. The altitude at which the tea was grown and the amount of rain and sunshine to which the crop was exposed are important factors. The time of the year the tea was harvested and any mishaps or delays in the withering, rolling, or drying process also affect quality.

To compensate for the variations in leaf quality and character, tea tasters blend many different teas, and this is what enables each of these firms to keep its product consistent in color, flavor, and aroma. A single tea bag, in fact, may contain as many as twenty or thirty different varieties of leaves from five or six different countries.

At one time, wholesalers blended tea so as to appeal to regional preferences. Oolongs, which are Chinese teas that are only partly fermented before drying, were preferred in New York, Pennsylvania, and most other states of the Eastern Seaboard. Japanese green teas were favored by people of the New England states, several Midwestern states, and in California. But regional preferences have all but disappeared. The great majority of tea drinkers today make their buying decisions on the basis of brand names. Lipton, Salada, and Tetley are the names with which people are now familiar, not oolong, souchong, or Darjeeling.

Teatasters decide how the different varieties of tea are to be blended. Tea tasting is an art. A taster sits at a table and carefully brews the teas to be evaluated in small white cups. He watches the leaves as they unfold. From time to time, he sniffs the aroma.

From each cup in turn, he takes a few wet leaves on a spoon, and judges them for color and aroma. Then he judges the liquid that has been brewed in each cup for color and aroma. Last, he tastes the liquid in each cup.

Professional teatasters of the 1870's

An expert in tea tasting can identify as many as fifteen hundred or sixteen hundred different teas. Many tasters have the ability to take a few dried leaves, crush them in their fingers, sniff them, and then tell you where they were grown, what variety of tea they are, at what season of the year they were picked, and how they were processed.

The blending is done in huge rotating drums. As the tea comes out of the drums, conveyor belts carry it to the packaging machines.

Tea bags are folded on machines . . . String is stapled on . . . Tea bag is inserted in envelope

SOUTHERN TEA COMPANY

The paper used in making the bags is of special quality. It has to be porous enough to allow the water to penetrate and infuse the leaves inside. It has to be strong enough to be able to survive being submerged in boiling water, not permitting a single leaf to escape.

The paper is supplied in big rolls and stored under carefully controlled conditions of temperature and humidity. It is not taken from the storage rooms until just before it is to be used in the packaging plant.

85

The most popular bags today are "flow-through" tea bags, sometimes called "2 in 1" bags. These are four-sided tea bags. They make for rapid brewing.

In making a flow-through tea bag, the first step is to measure out exactly the right amount of tea for each bag. The blended tea is fed through a chute into pockets that are mounted in what is called a dosing wheel. Each pocket holds just enough tea for one bag.

As the dosing wheel turns, it deposits tea from the pockets onto a moving strip of filter paper. The two sides of the strip of paper are then joined and crimped together, forming a continuous tube. The tube is cut into individual sections, each section containing its allotment of tea.

The bag's bottom pleat is then formed. The top is closed with a staple that also serves to trap one end of a length of string. To the other end of the string, a tag is attached.

The completed bag is inserted in an envelope. The small packets are then packaged in cartons. Each carton receives a heat-sealed outer wrapper of cellophane. This acts as a barrier to moisture, but it still permits the tea leaves to "breathe."

"Packaged tea retains six percent of its original moisture," an industry spokesman explains, "and this moisture could condense were the package to be completely air-tight." Condensation could lead to spoilage, of course.

The carton's cellophane wrap also guards the tea from odors produced by strong-smelling products, such as soap, that may be stacked nearby in the supermarket.

The latest development in tea packaging involves instant tea powders. These are sold in glass jars or foil packets.

And there are also tea mixes. These are instant teas which contain sugar or flavorings. During the summer months, instant teas combined with lemon flavoring for making iced tea sell in large quantities.

Nevertheless, the tea bag is still king. According to a recent survey by the Tea Council of the U.S.A., loose tea accounts for 6.9 percent of all marketed tea, instant tea mixes for 15.1 percent, instant tea itself for 29.7 percent, and tea bags for 48.3 percent.

Very few packages can point to a success record like that. If there were a Hall of Fame for convenience packaging, the tea bag would have to be a charter member.

8

INDUSTRY GIANT

HISTORY BOOKS DESIGNATE THE YEARS FROM 1792 TO 1800 as the period of the French Revolutionary Wars. French armies overran the Austrian Netherlands, crossed the Rhine into Germany, and seized Savoy and Nice from Sardinia. In Italy too one victory followed another.

But as the French penetrated deeper into foreign lands and their supply lines kept getting longer and longer, they began losing one battle after another to sickness and disease. There was no way to keep food fresh for extended periods of time in those days, and troops were made to subsist on a diet that consisted mainly of salted meat and dried bread. Without vitamins and minerals ordinarily provided by fruits and vegetables, many French soldiers contracted scurvy, a disease characterized by spongy and bleeding gums and extreme weakness.

In an effort to solve the problem, the French government offered a prize of twelve thousand francs to any citizen who could devise a method of processing food so that it would keep for long periods. The prize was won in 1810 by an obscure Parisian confectioner and chef named Nicolas Appert.

Believing that food spoilage was caused by air, Appert devised special methods for excluding it from his food containers, which were glass bottles and jars. His method of "canning" involved two steps. First, he immersed the filled containers in boiling water and kept them immersed until the food was thoroughly heated. The second step was to seal the containers airtight with corks.

Appert insisted upon corks of the highest quality. Using a wooden bat, he would hammer the corks into the bottle necks or jar mouths, then tie them down with wire. "In this manner," wrote Appert, "the bottle is perfectly corked on the outside as well as on the inside."

Appert had difficulty in getting corks that were big enough. When a particularly large stopper was needed, he would sometimes have to glue several corks together. Appert advised others who wished to try his process to buy their corks before buying jars or bottles. One could always find a glass container to fit a cork, but finding a cork for a container of a particular size could be a problem.

While the French government awarded Appert a gold medal as a "benefactor of humanity," and historians have come to regard him as one of the founders of the food-processing industry, Appert never really understood why his methods were successful. When occasional batches of foods that he had processed went bad, Appert blamed it on some failure in technique, on his inability to obtain a perfect seal. It is now believed that his failures were probably caused by the presence of certain microorganisms in the containers. The heat treatment that Appert used did not destroy these organisms. Not until the mid-1800's and the work of Louis Pasteur and others was it realized that the presence of certain microbes in food were what caused spoilage—it was not air.

About the same time that Nicolas Appert was winning the praise of the French government, an English merchant, one Peter Durand, applied to King George III for a patent covering a "Method of Preserving Animal Food, Vegetable Food, and Other Perishable Articles a Long Time from Perishing or Becoming Useless." Durand's experiments concerned containers not only of glass, but also of earthenware, tin, and what he called "other metals of fit materials."

It is believed that Durand sold his patent to John Hall,

founder of the Dartford Iron Works. That firm's tinsmiths are known to have made canisters out of thin strips of iron coated with tin. A good man could turn out as many as ten of these "cans" in a day.

Although the scientific reasons as to just why canning was successful were not fully understood, the process became well known in a relatively short span of time. The British navy is said to have discovered the advantages of canned foods in the early 1800's, and tinned beef became an item in regular issue by 1847. Otto Kotzebue, the Russian navigator and explorer, carried English canned foods with him in 1815 in his effort to find a passage across the Arctic Ocean.

A Boston, Massachusetts, cannery was processing jellies and jams, and currants and cranberries, as early as 1820. The canning of seafood in Maine began in 1854. Tomatoes were canned for students at Lafayette College in 1847.

An American inventor named Gail Borden received a patent for the canning of condensed milk in 1856 (see Chapter 4). Condensed milk is cow's milk but with sugar added. It has been reduced to a thick consistency by evaporation. During the Civil War, Borden's entire output of canned milk was used by the Northern armies.

An important breakthrough came in 1874, the year that A. K. Shriver of Baltimore invented the pressure cooker, a device that modern food processors refer to as a retort. The retort enables canners to produce and carefully control very high temperatures while cooking the sealed containers.

With the invention of the pressure cooker, canning plants began to spring up in every part of the country. Vegetable canneries were built in Iowa. A salmon cannery went into operation in Alaska in 1878, and peas were first canned in Wisconsin in 1881. The first pineapple cannery in Hawaii went into operation in 1892.

Today, the canning industry is a giant industry, with 1,700 canning plants in forty-nine of the fifty states producing 1,400 different items. These include vegetables and fruits, juices and juice drinks, seafoods and meats, and such specialties as soup, infant foods, and puddings.

What are the most popular canned foods? Among canned vegetables, these are the most popular:

1. Tomatoes
2. Corn
3. Green beans
4. Green peas
5. Beets
6. Sauerkraut
7. Asparagus
8. Sweet potatoes
9. Spinach
10. Carrots

A canning factory of the 1870's

As for canned fruits, here is a list of the top ten:

1.	Peaches	6.	Apricots
2.	Apples and applesauce	7.	Cranberry sauce
3.	Pineapples	8.	Olives
4.	Mixed fruits	9.	Citrus fruits
5.	Pears	10.	Plums

The term "canning" applied to the process used to preserve foods in sealed containers. It doesn't matter whether the container happens to be made of metal or glass—in each instance the canning methods are virtually the same.

Tin cans are not made of tin, as most people realize. They are made of sheet steel that is coated with tin. The can metal is usually 98 to 99.75 percent steel, in fact.

The use of cans in food packaging dates to the early 1800's. The first cans were made of tin plate. Sheets of iron were heated and rolled paper thin, then coated with tin.

Rectangles of tin plate were then formed into cylinders, and the circular tops and bottoms were soldered into place. Soldering is a process by which metal parts are joined by raising the temperature of each to its melting point. Since tin—and tinplate—has a relatively low melting point, it lends itself to this process.

A hole about $1\frac{1}{2}$ inches in diameter would be left in the can top. The food would be forced through the hole. When the can was filled, a patch would be soldered over the hole to close it.

To open such a can, one used a hammer and a small chisel, prying off the metal patch. The key-wind metal tear strip, which is common to some canned meats today, was introduced in 1866. The can opener, which got to be as common in the American home as running water, did not arrive until 1875.

In the early stages of the industry, can makers turned out about sixty cans a day. But by 1900 automatic machinery had been developed which was capable of

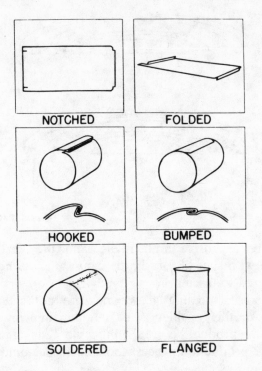

NOTCHED   FOLDED

HOOKED   BUMPED

SOLDERED   FLANGED

Cans are manufactured in this sequence of operations

AMERICAN CAN CO.

manufacturing twenty-five hundred cans an hour.

Soldered-end cans eventually gave way to those in which the top and bottoms were welded on or cemented on. But with some canned products, soldering persists. The condensed milk can is the most notable example.

When making a can today, the manufacturer begins with a rectangular piece of sheet steel, which has been notched on one end. The opposing ends of the rectangle are folded over, then hooked to one another. The two hooked ends are then crimped together, an operation known as "bumping." Last, the joint is sealed by welding, soldering, or the use of special cement.

Although Appert used glass jars in demonstrating the practicality of his canning method, the use of jars by commercial processors was slow to develop. Early glass

93

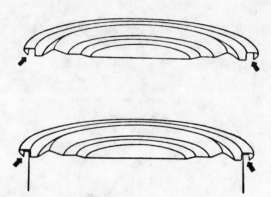

Inside curl of lid fixes onto can flange

jars were expensive and fragile, and they had to be handled with special care in the cannery and when being transported to the market.

Methods of sealing glass jars were not satisfactory, either. Another problem was that the time involved in cooling the product before the lid could be fastened down made the production process too slow to be commercially profitable.

Up until the 1930's, only a relatively small number of foods were to be found in vacuum packs. These included pickles, dried beef, nut meats, and hard candy. The one thing that all of these products had in common was that

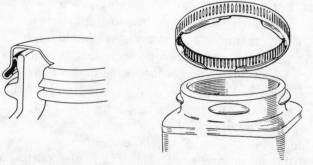

A pry-off lid (left) *and the lug type*

94

they did not require "hot filling," to use a processor's term.

A small vacuum chamber, about the size of a bread box, was used in packaging such foods. Once the jar had entered the chamber, the air was pumped out. The lid was then automatically applied to the jar and it was removed from the chamber.

A common lid of the time, and one frequently seen today, was made of metal and featured an angled rim or skirt which fitted over the jar rim. A rubber gasket was mounted on the inside face of the rim. Once the lid had been pressed into place and the jar removed from the chamber, outside air pressure held it tightly in place.

To open the jar, the consumer pried off the top. The package could be partly resealed by pressing the top back on.

A breakthrough in the processing of hot-packed foods came in 1929. That year William P. White was granted a patent that described a simple and clever method for obtaining a vacuum pack, but without the use of a vacuum chamber or the necessity of waiting for the product to cool before the cap was applied.

White instructed that the hot-filled jars not be filled completely, but to within only an inch or so of the top. The space remaining, called "headspace," was then filled with dry steam which displaced the air.

The cap was then immediately applied, trapping the steam. As the jar cooled, the steam condensed, creating the vacuum.

This development triggered a period of enormous growth in the packaging of food in glass containers. Green beans and tomatoes, peaches, peas, and cherries— virtually any fruit or vegetable—could be vacuum-packed in glass. Prices for such products dropped from luxury levels to within a range that appealed to the economy-minded housewife of the 1930's.

The packaging of food in glass containers received another important boost during World War II, when the United States was unable to obtain sufficient tin from the

Cans are delivered for filling at a California cannery

tin-producing countries of Asia to make metal cans. Canners and consumers turned to glass-packed foods as a result.

Glass containers, like metal cans, are manufactured by automatic machines. Molten glass is gathered in a mold having the same shape as the finished container, then blown to shape by compressed air. Modern machines are capable of producing bottles or jars at the rate of from ten to sixty a minute, depending upon the container's size and weight.

. . .

96

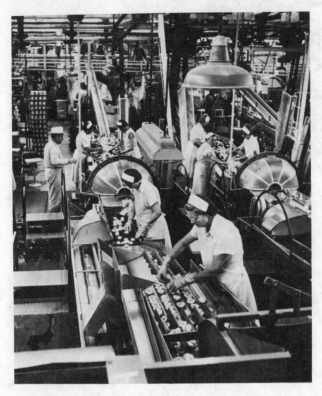

Yellow cling peaches are prepared for canning

DEL MONTE CORPORATION

While canning practices vary somewhat depending on the type of food involved, certain basic operations are common to all canned foods.

In the case of fruits and vegetables, the first step is washing, either by high-pressure sprays or rapid-flowing streams of water. Sorting is next. In sorting for size, the product is passed over moving screens of various mesh sizes. Separating the product according to degrees of ripeness usually has to be done by hand. But peas and lima beans are floated in a salt solution—the riper ones rise to the top.

After sorting, the product is trimmed. During this stage, the product may be peeled, sliced, diced, or halved. There

97

Cans of peaches make their way along the filling line
DEL MONTE CORPORATION

are machines that perform almost all of these chores. For example, after corn is received at the cannery, it is automatically husked and washed. Then special machines cut the corn from the cob. In canning whole kernel corn, the machine's knives are set to cut the kernels close to the cob. For cream-style corn the knives cut off only the kernel tops.

Some foods have to be blanched, a processing step in which they are immersed in hot water or subjected to a hot-steam bath. Blanching shrinks and wilts the food, as in the case of spinach, so that a greater quantity can be packed into the container. Blanching also drives out gases the product might contain, which could prove troublesome once the container is sealed. In addition, the process inactivates enzymes that can cause changes in food flavor.

98

This filling machine is called a "merry-go-round" unit
DEL MONTE CORPORATION

After these preparatory steps, the food to be canned pours into filling machines, and is then fed into the cans or jars. With whole peaches, pears, and some other foods, the containers are hand filled.

Before the lid is sealed onto the container, air is removed from it, that is, a vacuum is created. The vacuum helps to retain the natural color and appearance of the food and improves its keeping qualities. To obtain a vacuum, processors may use a vacuum chamber or employ the technique devised by William P. White. Both methods are described earlier in this chapter.

In sealing lids on metal cans, the curl of the lid interlocks with the flange of the can. An airtight seal is the result. Glass containers are sealed with a close-fitting cover, a threaded cap, or a lug cap.

Once sealed in its container, the product is ready to be cooked. Most fruits are processed at a temperature of 212° F. A conveyor belt carries the containers to a retort. Once the containers are inside the retort, the chamber is sealed shut.

99

Hot water or steam quickly fills the retort, driving out the air. Within a minute or two, the food within the cans reaches the desired cooking temperature. It remains at that temperature for a specified period of time.

The higher the cooking temperature, the shorter the cooking time. For instance, a can of cream-style corn can be processed in 85 minutes at 240° F. But the processing time can be reduced to 65 minutes if the temperature is raised to 250° F.

After the food is cooked, the retort is opened and the cans are conveyed to a cooling canal. If the cans are not cooled immediately after heat processing, the food inside continues to cook, and the quality can suffer.

The final step is to label the containers and pack them into shipping cartons.

Modern processing plants can fill, seal, label, and pack containers at the rate of 1,200 per minute. That type of production surely would have astonished Nicolas Appert, and probably could have made the French Revolutionary forces one of the most formidable armies of all times.

9

KEEPING THE CHEW
IN GUM

SUGAR. GUM BASE. CORN SYRUP. DEXTROSE. SOFTENERS. Natural flavors. These are the ingredients that go into making chewing gum. They're listed on the package label.

Together they make up a product that must have just the right texture. It can't be too soft, it can't be too brittle.

It has to be full of flavor, too.

Gum always has these qualities when it leaves the manufacturing plant. Whether it has them when you buy the product depends on the package.

The package has to be able to protect the gum against heat and humidity. It must also have the ability to keep the gum from drying out. And it has to be able to do this not only while the gum is on display awaiting purchase, but also during the time it is being shipped and stored. Several weeks, even many months, can be involved.

Actually, stick gum represents only one type of chewing gum. It is the most popular type, however.

There is also bubble gum. Bazooka is the most successful brand. Brightly wrapped in red, white, and blue paper, with a comic strip—Bazooka Joe—inside, Bazooka is chewed by young people in fifty-five different countries of the world.

A single thin slab of bubble gum is frequently sold in a packet with baseball cards. In one recent year the Topps Chewing Gum Company of Brooklyn, New York, sold more than a quarter of a billion baseball cards. That helps to explain why there are now also cards that feature football, basketball, and hockey players.

Candy-coated gum—Chiclets is the best-known brand —is second to stick gum in popularity. Candy-coated gum also refers to ball gum, the type available in automatic vending machines.

No matter which type of gum is involved, processing methods are about the same in each case. The ingredients that go into making the gum are brought to the manufacturing plant in big tank trucks and railroad cars to be stored in huge tanks, silos, and bins. Electronic consoles control the flow of ingredients from these various storage facilities into the plant mixers and other processing equipment.

The ingredient that is listed on the package as "gum base" is what puts the chew in the gum. Companies that manufacture gum from synthetic ingredients use polyvinyl acetate as a gum base. But the firms that prefer to use natural ingredients derive gum base from chicle, the milky liquid obtained from the sapodilla and other trees that grow in the steaming rain forests of Central America.

The sapodilla grows straight and tall, up to eighty feet in height. Workers who tap the trees are known as *chicleros*. The *chiclero* climbs to the top of the tree and then, using a large, heavy flat-bladed knife, he slices a series of connecting gashes down the tree's trunk. The sap flows steadily down the length of the tree to be collected in a canvas bag at the base. The average tree is capable of giving off two to three pounds of sap daily for three or four months of the year.

At a central camp, the juice is strained to remove some of the impurities, and then it is boiled. When the boiling

Packages of Bazooka, world's most popular bubble gum, stream from the wrapping machine

TOPPS CHEWING GUM, INC.

102

sap begins to thicken, the juice is poured into wooden molds and allowed to cool and harden. The blocks that result, each of which weighs about twenty-five pounds, are loaded onto mules and carried to the nearest seaport for shipment to the United States.

Resin, a liquidy substance obtained by tapping pine trees, is another ingredient that goes into the manufacture of gum base. The pines that produce resin are found in North Carolina, South Carolina, Georgia, Florida, Alabama, Mississippi, Louisiana, and Texas.

The ingredient listed on the gum label as "softeners" refers to a product made of refined vegetable oils. Softeners help in the blending of the ingredients that make up the gum base. They also add to the keeping quality of the gum. Sugar and corn syrup are used to enhance the gum's flavor and texture.

When it comes to gum flavor, Americans prefer various kinds of mint. Spearmint flavor is derived from a liquid extracted from farm-grown spearmint plants. Peppermint flavor comes from a similar plant. These flavors are also available in artificial form. Synthetic flavors, such as the Wrigley Company's "Juicy Fruit," are prepared from carefully guarded formulas.

The first step in manufacturing gum is to blend together the ingredients that go to make up the gum base. After the ingredients have been thoroughly mixed, the base is melted in huge steam-jacketed kettles. Next, the mixture is strained through fine mesh screens and rotated in centrifugal machines. These steps cleanse the mix of its impurities. At this stage, the base looks like thick maple syrup.

The gum base is then poured into giant mixers, each capable of holding two thousand pounds. Carefully measured amounts of powdered sugar, corn syrup, and flavoring are added. Big rotary blades mix the ingredients together.

When the mixing is completed, the gum passes between rollers that press it into an endless ribbon that is about two

104

Picture card bubble gum gets a single wax wrapper

TOPPS CHEWING GUM, INC.

and one-half inches thick. After the ribbon has been allowed to cool, kneading machines press, fold, and stretch it.

The gum ribbon then moves through several pairs of rollers, each pair reducing its thickness. After the final rolling, the ribbon has exactly the thickness of a stick of gum. The ribbon is then cut into rectangular sheets, each one about twice the size of this page.

The sheets are fed one by one into a "breaking" machine. With one quick click, each sheet is cut into twenty-two sticks of gum. A single machine can "break" 3,330 sticks in a minute.

Now the gum is ready to be packaged. Gum sticks are first wrapped in tissue paper. The paper is waxed on the inside and coated with foil on the outside. Then each stick is inserted in a printed paper sleeve.

The sticks are then fed into an automatic wrapping machine, which gathers seven sticks at a time (or five sticks, or seventeen, depending on the size of the package) and overwraps them in a three-ply printed wrapper. The wrapper's inner layer is foil, and its outer layer is cellophane. Sandwiched in between is waxed paper.

Before sending the packaged gum on its way to be boxed, the wrapping machine seals the ends of each package.

Bubble gum does not get nearly so much packaging protection as stick gum. A simple waxed-paper wrapper is all that is used.

I asked a spokesman for a major bubble-gum company why this was so. He shrugged. "Our customers," he said, "really aren't too concerned about flavor and texture. What they're interested in is the cards they're getting and how big a bubble they can blow."

10

THE REVOLUTION

SOMETIMES A NEW PACKAGE WILL HAVE A STARTLING EF-fect upon an individual product. Putting hair sprays in aerosol cans sent sales skyrocketing.

Occasionally a package will shake an entire industry. The tea bag, for instance.

And then there are those very rare cases where a form of packaging will cause revolutionary change in the nation's habits. That's what frozen-food packaging did, and is continuing to do.

Frozen foods used to mean chiefly vegetables and fruits, but today the list includes fruit drinks, fish and seafood, meat and poultry, and many different types of bakery goods. Not a year goes by that the list doesn't get a little bit longer.

The commercial freezing of food dates to 1891, when frozen mutton was transported from New Zealand to England. A "cold pack" method of freezing was intro-duced in the United States in 1905. Berries, after being washed and sorted, were placed in barrels and frozen in ice-cold storage.

The process took days. Besides being very slow, there was a marked change in the berries' color, texture, and appearance. They could be used in making jams, jellies, and bakery products, but that was about all. You wouldn't want to eat them on breakfast cereal.

To protect against loss of quality, products had to be

Green beans, eight tons of them, arrive at the processing plant
GENERAL FOODS CORPORATION

quick-frozen. The commercial quick-freezing process was pioneered by Clarence Birdseye. In the early 1920's, he developed a cumbersome but workable machine that could quick-freeze fish. The packaged fish moved between two stainless-steel belts while being sprayed with cold brine. Mr. Birdseye's patents and equipment were purchased in 1929 by the Postum Company (now General Foods Corporation).

Frozen foods were put on sale on a test basis in ten grocery stores in Springfield, Massachusetts, in 1930. While the test was successful, it was another fifteen years before frozen foods were readily accepted by American consumers, and it was not until the mid-1950's that frozen-food production began to attain the importance it has today.

. . .

Foods are prepared for freezing in much the same way that they are prepared for canning (Chapter 8). Take green beans as an example. After the beans are harvested, they are trucked to the frozen-food processing plant for inspection, grading, washing, and trimming.

Then the beans are blanched, as described earlier. All vegetables are blanched.

After blanching, the beans are quickly cooled in a stream of ice water. Now they are ready for freezing.

There are many different types of freezing available to food processors, and new ones are constantly being developed. Plate freezing is based on Clarence Birdseye's experiments. In this process, packaged foods are placed on hollow metal shelves, or "plates," through which a liquid refrigerant is circulated. Plate freezing is used for asparagus, cauliflower, spinach, broccoli, and other irregularly shaped foods, all of which must be packaged before the freezing.

A more recent process involves the use of freezing

Beans are inspected and graded

GENERAL FOODS CORPORATION

tunnels. This method is used for packaged meats, poultry, and bakery goods, as well as some packaged fruits and vegetables. The packages are stacked on trays which are then loaded onto dollies or hand trucks. The trucks are rolled into a tunnel where big fans or blowers keep cold air circulating. After a few hours, the packages are frozen solid.

A variation of this system is conveyor-tunnel freezing. Such vegetables as green peas, cut corn, and green and yellow beans are piled several inches deep on a conveyor belt that carries them into a freezing zone where air cooled to $-35°$ F is being circulated. Freezing takes only a matter of minutes.

Cut and blanched beans fall from a shaker screen to enter a tunnel freezer

GENERAL FOODS CORPORATION

Quick-frozen onions, carrots, and corn drop from a chute (left) *onto a circular filling machine. Brush sweeps the vegetables through circular openings into the cartons*

GENERAL FOODS CORPORATION

Another recently developed method of freezing vegetables of this type involves freezing them when they are in motion, while they are falling through the freezing zone instead of being conveyed through it. When green peas, for example, are frozen using this method, each pea is frozen separately. The processor then stores the peas. Packaging is done later.

This is known as the IQF (for individually quick frozen) process. One advantage of the IQF method is that it enables the processor to handle more of the crop during peak harvest periods. Once he's through freezing, he assigns his labor force to start packaging. Foods frozen in this manner are packaged in plastic-film bags.

The IQF process also benefits the homemaker. Since the peas are individually frozen, not frozen in a solid block, one simply pours out the quantity needed and returns the remainder to the freezer for later use.

Another new technique in commercial freezing makes use of cryogenics, the science of very low temperatures.

111

Beef, seafood, and poultry are being frozen cryogenically, as are pizza and onion rings.

The cryogenic process involves subjecting the products to temperatures of $-75°$ F, and even below. Ultra-fast freezing is the result, which assures better flavor, color, and texture.

Packaging line at a Woodburn, Oregon, food-freezing plant. In foreground filled cartons are being checked to determine whether weights are correct

GENERAL FOODS CORPORATION

112

A decade ago, there were thirty-five cryogenic freezing plants in operation in the United States. The number is now approaching ten times that.

Just as food-freezing techniques have changed in recent years, so have packaging methods and materials. The traditional frozen-food package was the paperboard carton with a waxed paper outer wrap. That's still very much in use, of course, but frozen foods are also being packaged in foil-lined cylinders, plastic cylinders, foil pouches, and vacuum pouches of plastic film.

The many changes in frozen-food processing and packaging have worked to transform the frozen-food section of the American supermarket. The early store freezer cabinet was small, not much bigger than a steamer trunk, and it was equipped with a cumbersome lid that had to be opened to remove or even look at the food packages. Today's shopper selects frozen foods from handsome multi-tiered units, completely open in front. Temperature is maintained by the use of an "air curtain." Right inside the "curtain" there's likely to be a thermometer to show the customer that the temperature is zero or below.

The amount of store display space given over to frozen foods is also getting bigger all the time.

The same sort of change has taken place in the home refrigerator. The modern refrigerator has a compartment that holds sufficient frozen food to last a family for a week or more. In addition, more than a third of all American households are equipped with big freezer chests.

Not long ago, the frozen-food industry conducted a survey to determine consumer attitudes toward frozen foods. People buy frozen products, it was found, because, first, they're easy to prepare; second, they're good-tasting; third, they're good nutritionally; fourth, they're a good value. When so much is in their favor, the revolution in frozen foods seems certain to keep going on and on.

11
Sssssssssst

A CONVENIENCE, SAYS THE DICTIONARY, IS ANYTHING THAT is handy or easy to use, anything that saves trouble or work. When it comes to convenience packaging, nothing fits that description better than the aerosol.

The term "aerosol" refers to a type of container that holds any one of a variety of products—hair sprays and shaving creams, paints and household cleansers, perfumes and body powders—under pressure with a gaseous propellant. The container valve is capable of releasing the product as a spray, foam, or even as a dust.

During the 1960's the consuming public found aerosols to be so wonderfully "convenient" that these containers became an industry in themselves. Hundreds of different aerosol products were sold under thousands of different labels. It was the push-button era of packaging.

Today, the picture is anything but rosy. Some aerosols have been accused of being the cause of serious environmental damage. The aerosol industry says it is not guilty. Scientists the world over are now at work in an attempt to resolve the issue.

. . .

There's nothing complex about an aerosol container and the way in which it dispenses its product. Within the sturdily built container one finds the product to be dispensed, in liquid form, and pressing down upon it, a

114

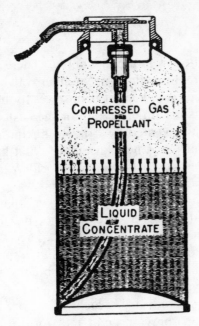

COMPRESSED GAS
PROPELLANT

LIQUID
CONCENTRATE

Compressed gas within the aerosol container exerts pressure on the liquid concentrate, forcing it into the dip tube. Valve at container top releases the product, usually in spray form

FOOD PROCESSING AND MARKETING

layer of compressed gas propellant.

What's called a dip tube, a slender nylon tube about the size and shape of a drinking straw, stretches from the valve at the container top into the liquid. When one presses down on the valve it opens the mouth of the dip tube, and the liquid surges up the tube and into the valve. There it is converted into its final form, usually a mist spray.

In addition to convenience, aerosols have other advantages. They don't spill. The product is always applied uniformly. And because the container is airtight, the contents are less susceptible to spoilage or deterioration.

New and improved aerosols are being planned for the years ahead. One is a cylinder-shaped container which holds propellant and is equipped with a dip tube and a valve. A separate detached glass bottle screws into the base of the cylinder.

Suppose the bottle holds hair spray. When the hair spray is used up, the bottle is simply unscrewed from the

115

cylinder and refilled from a bulk supply. There's no need to purchase more propellant or another valve and dip tube. Many liquids could adapt themselves to this system. It would mean a substantial saving for the customer.

The aerosol was invented by Erik Rothheim, a Norwegian, in 1924. But the American public's first knowledge of aerosols dates to the early years of World War II and a device that was called a "bug bomb." This was a ruggedly built, high-pressure container that looked like a small bomb. Fitted with a screw-thread spray nozzle, it dispensed an insecticide or insect repellent. The valve could be turned to an "on" position for continuous spraying, or turned on and off for quick spurts. Bug bombs were used by the armed services during the war.

The giant aerosol industry, which sells more than 150 billion push-button sprays around the world every year, got its start on the basis of a patent issued to L. D. Goodhue and W. N. Sullivan in 1943. Both men were employees of the U.S. Department of Agriculture at the time, so their patent was assigned to the Secretary of Agriculture for public use.

Many inventors developed aerosols on the basis of this patent, and in the years that followed World War II many of them were beginning to reach the marketplace. These aerosols were usually insecticides, mothproofers, or room deodorants.

But the dispensing system these aerosols relied upon was far from perfect. The chief problem was with the valve that regulated the flow of the spray. It frequently leaked or rusted, and when it rusted it stuck. For every three aerosols there were sold in those days, two were likely to be returned by the customer.

In the summer of 1949, an East Coast distributor of aerosol products explained the problem to Robert Abplanalp, the owner of a Bronx, New York, machine shop. "Could you design and manufacture an improved valve?" he asked.

Abplanalp said he would try. He began by taking apart

116

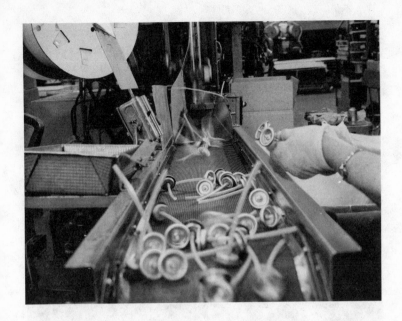

Valves stream off the assembly line

existing valves and cutting them up to learn how they were constructed. Having his own machine shop was a big advantage. When he wanted to test an idea, he would draw a sketch and then make the part himself, and he could do it all in a matter of hours. If the idea proved unsound, he could put it aside and try another tack.

One thing that hampered Abplanalp was a poor background in chemistry. He had to know the particle size of the various sprays with which he was dealing, and how corrosive each of them might be. A friend introduced him to a chemist who supplied him with much of the information he needed.

Container is spray-tested

117

Abplanalp's research met with success in very short time. In the fall of 1949, he introduced a new valve that overcame many of the problems of the old one. One important improvement was the introduction of a circular metal cup into which the valve was mounted. Previous valves had been soldered or welded right into the container top, and leaks were a frequent result.

The Abplanalp valve also featured a tapered valve stem. The gradual decrease in the stem diameter assured that the container would be sealed tightly when the valve was in a closed position.

Abplanalp formed a company with headquarters in Yonkers, New York, to manufacture and sell valves.

Machines like this one are used to test valve efficiency

Aerosols were a novelty at first, but within a few years the industry took on international importance. Manufacturing plants were established in Mexico, Canada, Argentina, Australia, South Africa, and several European countries. By the early 1970's, Abplanalp's firm, Precision Valve Corporation, was producing as many as five million valves a day.

. . . .

Aerosols have been in the headlines frequently in recent years. During the summer of 1974, F. Sherwood Rowland and Mario J. Molina, two chemists at the University of California at Irvine, published a study which stated that an element in the compound used to propel products from aerosol containers could be damaging the precious ozone layer that surrounds the earth.

The ozone layer is an area in which ozone gas is concentrated and which surrounds the earth at altitudes of from 50,000 to 115,000 feet. The greatest concentration is believed to be at 80,000 feet. The ozone layer serves to shield the earth from the sun's ultraviolet radiation. Should the layer be destroyed, or even diminished to a large extent, man could not survive. The world's population would suffer increased skin cancer. Possibly crops would be damaged. Some scientists say that any major depletion in the ozone layer would cause drastic changes in global climate. It could cause, for example, a new ice age, with glaciers thousands of feet thick covering Europe and North America.

Different gases are used by the aerosol industry as propellants, but usually they are either hydrocarbons or fluorocarbons. Hydrocarbons, which are cheaper than fluorocarbons, are not suspected of destroying the ozone layer. But hydrocarbons, when used with alcohol-based ingredients, result in a highly flammable product.

Aerosol shaving creams and many household products, such as paint and furniture polish, use hydrocarbons. But these products contain water, and the water serves to

119

overcome the flammability of the hydrocarbons.

About one half of all aerosols, as of 1975, used fluorocarbons as a propellant, and it is these that triggered the ozone controversy. Fluorocarbons are compounds of fluorine, chlorine, and carbon.

Fluorocarbons have been used as the propellants in most personal products—hair sprays, perfumes, and deodorants. They have also been used as propellants in most insecticides and air fresheners. Why do manufacturers use fluorocarbons? Because they reduce the flammability of the active ingredients, many of which contain large amounts of alcohol. If hydrocarbons were to be used with hair spray, for instance, the result would be a highly flammable product.

Late in 1975, nine states and three environmental groups petitioned the Consumer Product Safety Commission to ban the use of fluorocarbons in aerosol sprays. The petition cited research findings that tended to confirm the conclusions of Professors Rowland and Molina, and included evidence collected from high-altitude balloon tests conducted by the National Oceanic and Atmospheric Administration and the National Center for Atmospheric Research.

It must be said that the aerosol industry is not ready to agree that fluorocarbons are about to cause a global tragedy. One industry spokesman brands as "nonsense" the findings of Rowland and Molina. "All the scientific theories against fluorocarbons are just that—theories, not facts," he says. "We need more research."

That research is already under way. Several industry groups and private organizations, working with more than a dozen different universities, are conducting scientific investigations to gain additional data on fluorocarbon gases and their effects, if any, on the upper atmosphere. The results may not be known for years, however.

No matter what type of propellant it contains, any aerosol must be treated with respect. Always read the label before you press the button.

120

Anytime you use an aerosol, keep the spray away from your face. If heavy spraying is necessary, be sure that the room in which you are spraying is well ventilated.

Aerosols should be kept away from heat. Never leave an aerosol container on a hot stove, near a furnace or radiator, or in the hot sun.

When the container is empty, dispose of it with non-burnable trash. Never throw an empty container into an incinerator or open fire.

.   .   .

With aerosols under attack, the packaging industry is turning to several other dispensing systems that offer somewhat the same features as the aerosol. One of these is the mechanical pump spray. During 1975, pump-spray manufacturers worked at top speed to meet the increased demand for their product from the makers of cosmetics, toiletries, and a variety of household products.

The pump spray uses mechanical energy supplied by the user, who presses straight down on a small handle mounted directly above the container top. Continued up and down pressure forces the product into a dip tube and out through a spray valve.

The pump dispenser is not new. It has been in use since the 1940's, but it is only in recent years that it has attained widespread use. It is a less than perfect system, however. Pumps can dispense only relatively thin liquids, although this problem is likely to be solved through research.

Cost is a more serious problem. A pump dispenser costs about 20 cents, an aerosol valve only about 3½ cents.

Meanwhile, the controversy concerning fluorocarbons and the ozone layer continues. Whatever the outcome, though, not all aerosols are going to be affected. You can be sure that *Sssssssssst* is a sound that is going to continue to be heard for many years to come.

12

HOW TO GET RID OF IT?

OVER 400 BILLION PACKAGES ARE USED EACH YEAR IN the United States. This includes 62 billion metal cans, 35 billion glass bottles, and 7 billion plastic bottles. It also includes additional billions of cardboard cartons and cases, and plastic bags and wrappings.

As these statistics suggest, packaging wastes have become an enormous problem. It is now estimated that the average American household generates about a ton of trash each year.

While packaging wastes represent only a part of this amount, it is a big enough part to have angered more than a few environmentally concerned citizens. One effect has been that well over half the state legislatures in this country have conducted hearings on bills that would restrict the marketing of certain types of packages or packages made of certain materials. Legislation passed in the state of Oregon in 1972 made it mandatory that a five-cent deposit be placed on all nonrefillable beverage containers. This resulted in the removal of all one-trip bottles from the state's supermarkets and substantially reduced the number of beer and soft-drink cans, which also had to be returned to get one's nickel back. The law was aimed at reducing roadside litter.

A new law in Minnesota gives a state board the authority to pass on every new package introduced in the state and to accept or ban it on the basis of its anticipated effect on the environment.

Legislation against packaging that has harmful environmental effects has been considered on a national level too. Late in 1975, Senator Mark O. Hatfield of Oregon proposed a bill that would eliminate detachable openings on cans and require a deposit on all beverage containers within one year from the law's enactment.

The packaging industry admits that it helps to generate

Apple juice is one product that is packaged in a reusable container
GEORGE SULLIVAN

123

"substantial amounts" of trash. But it points out that eliminating some forms of packaging would not eliminate the waste problem.

Take frozen French fried potatoes, for example. The potatoes are washed mechanically at the processing plant, then peeled. They are not peeled with a knife, the way the housewife performs the chore. Instead, they are "lye-peeled." Lye, also known as caustic soda, is used to "burn" the peels away. It's a much more efficient method, producing only ten or fifteen percent as much waste as when potatoes are knife-peeled.

After the potatoes are trimmed and cut, they are fried quickly under carefully controlled conditions. Freezing and packaging are the final steps.

When it comes to using the product, the consumer simply reheats the potatoes. The only waste generated is the package or pouch that contained the product.

The waste that accumulates in processing, the peels and the trimmed-away portions, is trucked away and used as cattle feed. Had the homemaker peeled and trimmed the potatoes herself, the waste would have ended up in what experts in the field refer to as the "solid waste system." Solid waste is trash. It's anything dumped in the garbage can.

"Each year," says a recently published study, "the processing industry generates about 10 million tons of waste in processing raw products. However, 7.3 million tons of this waste are recycled, primarily as animal feed." These figures refer to canned, frozen, and dehydrated fruits, vegetables, and seafoods.

"If these foods were not processed and packaged," the report continues, "the peels, husks, pits, cobs, and the like, still would have to be removed, but they would have to be removed in homes or restaurants." In other words, there would be little or no opportunity for economic recycling.

Packaged processed foods are also said to reduce waste because they cut spoilage. Some fruits and vegetables inevitably spoil in the time it takes to transport them from

124

the field to the supermarket. Fresh meat, poultry, and seafood are also subject to spoilage. Waste also results when the fresh products remain in the home refrigerator for too long a period.

Food-processing plants are located within or at least adjacent to growing areas. Fruit, vegetables, and other perishables are in transit for only brief periods. Losses because of spoilage are rare.

The food processor also helps to reduce waste by using odd-sized, undersized, or otherwise defective fruits and vegetables. They usually go toward making juices. Even fruits or vegetables that have been affected by mildew or insects can sometimes be used. The defective portion is trimmed away and the rest of the product salvaged.

One way that the packaging industry is helping to reduce the amount of waste that does occur is by

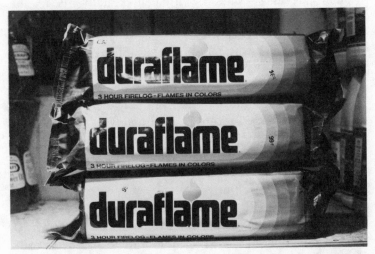

With this "firelog," the package gets burned up along with the product

GEORGE SULLIVAN

125

innovative package design. The best-known example is the reusable bottle, jar, or plastic tub. When the housewife buys a quart of apple juice, say, the empty glass bottle is likely to wind up, not in the household trash, but in the refrigerator as a storage bottle. The bottle and its cap have been designed to be reused.

The packaging used for charcoal briquettes, those lumps of charcoal used in outdoor grills, does not present any environmental problem either. The package wrapper is meant to be burned up right along with the briquettes.

Similar in theory is the water-soluble package. It takes the form of a small sack made of polyvinyl film which dissolves in cold water in three seconds. It's the ideal package for products which are used in water solutions. Filled with powdered soap or detergent, the package enables the housewife to put into her washer exactly the right amount of the product without measuring.

Manufacturers of insecticides also use such packages. They can be dissolved in spraying-machine tanks. The machine operator never has to touch the liquid.

Such packages could be used in restaurants in the brewing of coffee or in the preparation of soups made from dehydrated vegetables.

Obviously, boilaway bags and reusable glass bottles are not going to solve the nation's trash problem. Their contribution, in fact, is hardly noticeable.

The packaging industry itself tends to believe that it is not the proper target of those concerned with the problems associated with the daily accumulations of trash and garbage. It is more logical, say industry spokesmen, to point to the trash collection and disposal methods practiced by most communities.

In the earliest of times, man simply threw his refuse— broken pottery, shells, and bones—wherever he liked. If the trash accumulated and became a nuisance, he moved. The cliff dwellers living in the caves of Mesa Verde, Colorado, tossed rubbish from their caves. In time, enormous trash heaps sloped right up to the cave mouth.

Recycling centers are one answer to the trash problem

GEORGE SULLIVAN

127

To a great extent this practice, called "open dumping," is still in use today. Dumps are unsightly, have a bad odor, and are a breeding ground for rodents and disease organisms. Whereas ancient man could walk away from his trash heap, modern man can't. You can't move entire cities.

Ocean dumping is another traditional trash-disposal method. Solid waste is loaded aboard barges and dumped in offshore waters. But this practice has recently been recognized as environmentally hazardous, and it is declining.

There are several reasonable alternatives to open dumping and ocean dumping. One is the conversion of open

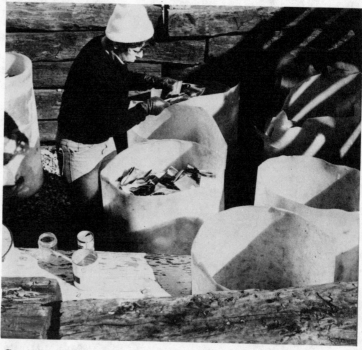

Sorting metal cans for recycling

GEORGE SULLIVAN

128

dumps to sanitary landfills. In operating a sanitary landfill, the refuse is compacted and buried as it is dumped on the land. It is a simple and relatively inexpensive method for handling the growing volume of rubbish. It has the added benefit of creating a community asset, a public park or residential land. It can be sloped to create a ski area or a golf course.

But not every city has land that can be used for fill. San Francisco, surrounded on three sides by water, must already haul its trash out of the area. New York City has almost run out of landfill space.

The municipal incinerator is a second alternative to open dumping. About two hundred American cities use this method of trash disposal. It's expensive to build and operate an incinerator and it is not a complete disposal method. Ash and other residue from the burning process must be disposed of.

The best solution is not to get rid of the rubbish at all, but to reprocess it and reuse it. For example, recovered container glass is being used in the manufacture of certain building materials and in a road paving material called glasphalt. This is ordinary asphalt in which crushed bottles replace crushed limestone. Fibers recovered from wastepaper can be used in the manufacture of roofing felt. Of course, they can also be reprocessed to make new paper. Food waste can be converted into compost and used to enrich the land.

With some materials, particularly metals, the recycling rate is already very high. In one recent year, sixty-one percent of all the copper available for recycling was, in fact, recycled. The rate for aluminum was forty-eight percent, and for nickel, forty percent.

But with most of the materials that make up solid wastes the percentage is dismally low. Only nineteen percent of the paper available for recycling ever gets recycled, and in recent years the percentage has been dropping. Glass is another material of which very little gets reclaimed.

In many communities, citizens have organized voluntary recycling centers to which individuals can bring discarded bottles, cans, paper, and other materials with salvage value. Some industries are supporting these centers by providing a market for the salvage.

But industry experts agree that such recycling centers are only the beginning. The recovery and reuse of valuable materials from municipal wastes depends upon the development of commercial systems that will serve the entire community.

The National Center for Resources Recovery, established in 1970, is spearheading development of what it refers to as "total recovery plants." These would reclaim the reusable elements found in solid wastes and, in addition, provide a source of fuel for power plants.

The system would work like this: The plant takes in unmixed household wastes directly from collection trucks and runs it through an ingenious combination of shredders, sorters, and pollution-free incinerators. In the first stage, nonferrous metals, aluminum, and glass are recovered.

What remains is pyrolyzed, that is, consumed in heat in the near absence of oxygen. This produces some worthwhile by-products, including gas, oil, and charcoal. All that is left is a black, gritty substance which can be used in the construction of roadbeds.

Officials in New York City have estimated that if the 30,000 tons of refuse generated in the city each day could be handled in this fashion, it would produce fifteen percent of the city's electricity needs. Moreover, it would result in a saving of 506 million gallons of fuel oil a year.

Recovery systems are already in operation in some areas. In Franklin, Ohio, the Environmental Protection Agency has helped to construct a plant that is capable of recovering paper and ferrous metals from municipal solid waste. The plant is designed to process up to 150 tons of waste per day. It has been in operation since 1971.

Incoming refuse is funneled into a huge mixer called a hydrapulper which converts paper, cardboard, and plastics

130

into a soupy mix that is known as slurry. Large, heavy objects are removed from the hydrapulper through an opening in the bottom.

A magnet separates the metal from the slurry, and then it is pumped through a liquid cyclone which removes glass, sand, and small pieces of metal. The glass is later sorted by means of a color scanner. (Glass manufacturers are unwilling to use bottle glass in the making of new glass unless it is all one color.) Aluminum is also removed from the slurry.

All recoverable fibers are dried and then baled. The water is removed from the sludge, and any solid particles that remain are incinerated.

Many recovery systems now in operation are based to a large extent upon incineration. Chicago, for example, has developed a recovery system for some of its refuse that utilizes a huge four-burner incinerator that is capable of handling 1,600 tons of refuse a day. Except for large and very bulky items, such as a washer, stove, or other major appliance, the refuse is fed into the incinerator in an "as received" state by loading it upon an inclined ramp which produces a constant downward flow. Metals are removed magnetically. A unique feature of the plant is that some of the steam it generates is used to power the operation of the incinerator, while the rest is sold to commercial clients.

What these paragraphs mean is that a beginning has been made. But it's only a beginning. Packaging's problem is nowhere near being solved.

The conveniences provided by packaging are one of the features of modern American life. The price the nation pays is a growing volume of rubbish, and there are few signs that consumers wish to change things. Indeed, the opposite is true, for there is a growing demand for more convenience foods, for more "throwaway" packaging.

And there is the industry itself, the manufacturers of paperboard, metal cans, glass containers, plastics, and all the rest. They have no wish to produce less. Lobbyists representing these and other segments of the packaging

131

industry wield enormous power, constantly beating back attempts on both the state and federal levels to limit package production in any way. For instance, efforts to restrict the use of throwaway bottles, replacing them with returnable, reusable bottles, never fail to be enthusiastically resisted by the glass-container industry.

The solution to the problem probably lies in the development of more efficient systems for the handling of waste materials, systems similar to those cited above, which provide for the recovery and eventual reuse of metals, paper, glass, and the rest. But less packaging? It's not likely.

ACKNOWLEDGMENTS

John Anderson
Tea Council of the U.S.A.

Jerry Arkebauer
Owens-Illinois, Inc.

Vincent Carberry
Precision Valve Corp.

J. Rodney Edwards
American Paper Institute

Frank Goodman
Southern Tea Co.

Mary R. Hoban
Nabisco

Eddie Jurman
D'Agostino's

Kathleen Keller
Del Monte Corp.

Ted Klein
Metal Tube Packaging Council of North America

Aime LaMontagne, Jr.
Stop & Shop, Inc.

Stephen Lion
Stephen Lion Associates

Marie McDermott
Thomas J. Lipton, Inc.

Connie Meehan
The Softness Group

William W. Menz
United Dairy Industry Ass'n

Robert Morrow
H. P. Hood & Sons

Barbara Noveau
American Frozen Food Institute

Steven Schwartz
Liss Public Relations

Timothy Sullivan
New York, N.Y.

William J. Sullivan
General Offset Printing Co.

William Taylor
General Foods Corp.

Gary Wagner
Wagner-International Photos

John B. Whitlock
Gerber Products Co.

Sally Wise
Glass Container Manufacturers Institute

J. J. Wuerthner, Jr.
Paperboard Packaging Council

133

BIBLIOGRAPHY

Chapter 1 CRACKER BOX, PACKAGING CLASSIC

Cahn, William, *Out of the Cracker Barrel: The Nabisco Story from Animal Crackers to ZuZus.* Simon & Schuster, Inc., 1969.

The Folding Carton. Washington, D.C.: Paperboard Packaging Council, 1969.

Forty Years of Paperboard Packaging Progress. Washington, D.C.: Paperboard Packaging Council, 1974.

"Reduce Folding Carton Costs by Judicious Structural Design," *Package Development,* July/August 1975.

Chapter 2 PrePACKAGING

Flexible Packaging: Facts and Fancies. Technical Report No. F-6528. The Packaging Institute, 1965.

"Flexible Packaging: Something for Everything," *Modern Packaging,* April 1967.

A History of Hot Melt Adhesives. Technical Report No. T-7002. The Packaging Institute, 1970.

Sacharow, Stanley, and Griffin, Roger C., *Food Packaging.* Westport, Connecticut: Avi Publishing Co., Inc., 1970.

Chapter 3 HOW DO THEY CLOSE IT?

Closure Committee, *Source Book for Closures.* The Packaging Institute, 1974.

A Food Packager Looks at High Speed Container and Cap Handling. Technical Report No. T-7107. The Packaging Institute, 1970.

Leif, Alfred, *A Close-Up of Closures.* Glass Container Manufacturers Institute, n.d.

Packaging in Glass. Toledo, Ohio: Glass Container Division, Owens-Illinois, Inc., 1974.

Chapter 4 MAKING MILK SAFE

A Fresh Look at Fresh Milk Packaging. Technical Report No. F-7043. The Packaging Institute, 1970.
New Trends in Dairy Packaging. Technical Report No. F-6904. The Packaging Institute, 1969.
Pouch Packaging for Milk. Technical Report No. F-6914. The Packaging Institute, 1969.

Chapter 5 A LITTLE SQUEEZE

The Story of the Metal Tube. New York: The Metal Tube Packaging Council of North America, 1969.
"Tube Filling for Viscous Products," *Tube Topics,* Vol. IX, November 4, 1975.

Chapter 6 BETTER BY DESIGN

Barail, Louis C., *Packaging Engineering.* Reinhold Publishing Corporation, 1954.
Newbauer, Robert G., *Packaging, the Contemporary Media.* Van Nostrand-Reinhold Company, 1973.

Chapter 7 A MATTER OF CONVENIENCE

"Getting Into More Hot Water Can Be Profitable," *Packages & People,* No. 2, 1971.
"Putting Tea to the Taste," *FDA Consumer,* September 1974.
Shalleck, Jamie, *Tea.* The Viking Press, Inc., 1972.
Ukers, William H., *All About Tea.* New York: The Tea and Coffee Trade Journal Company, 1935.

Chapter 8 INDUSTRY GIANT

The Canning Industry. 6th ed. Washington, D.C.: National Canners Association, 1971.
Desrosier, Norman W., *The Technology of Food Preservation.* Westport, Connecticut: Avi Publishing Co., Inc., 1970.
Leif, Alfred, *A Close-Up of Closures.* New York: Glass Containers Manufacturers Institute, n.d.

Chapter 9 KEEPING THE CHEW IN GUM

"Baseball Fans—and Gum Chewers, Too—Sing, 'You're the Topps,' " *The New York Times,* April 2, 1972.
Facts About Chewing Gum. Chicago: William Wrigley Jr., Co., n.d.
How Bazooka Is Made. Topps Chewing Gum, Inc., n.d.

Chapter 10 THE REVOLUTION

Facts About Frozen Foods. Chicago, Illinois: FACT, 1975.
The Frozen Food Industry in the United States: Its Origin, Development and Future, Frozen Foods Division, Pet Incorporated, 1973.

Chapter 11 SSSSSSSSSST

"Aerosol Feels the Ozone Effect," *The New York Times,* June 22, 1975.
"Patent on Precision's All-Purpose Valve Approaches Seventeenth Year," *Aerosol Age,* October 1968.
The Pushbutton Era in Convenience Packaging. Yonkers, New York: Precision Valve Corp., n.d.
Research Points Up Uncertainties in Fluorocarbon/Ozone Depletion Theory. New York: Council on Atmospheric Science, Aerosol Education Bureau, 1975.
"What We Do Know—and Don't Know—About the Ozone Shield," *Fortune,* August 1975.
"What's Being Done About Those Killer Aerosol Cans? Nothing," *New Times,* March 17, 1975.

Chapter 12 HOW TO GET RID OF IT?

Flexible Packaging and the Environment. Cleveland, Ohio: National Flexible Packaging Association, 1972.
Milgrom, Jack, and Brody, Aaron, *Packaging in Perspective.* A Report to the Ad Hoc Committee on Packaging. Cambridge, Massachusetts: Arthur D. Little, Inc., February 1974.
"Packaging: Who Needs It?" *Packaging Digest,* June 1974.

INDEX

139

141

142

143